The Breakthrough Challenge

The Breakthrough Challenge

10 Ways to Connect Today's Profits with Tomorrow's Bottom Line

John Elkington and Jochen Zeitz

Foreword by Sir Richard Branson

JB JOSSEY-BASS™

A Wiley Brand

Published by Jossey-Bass

A Wiley Brand

One Montgomery Street, Suite 1200, San Francisco, CA 94104-4594 — www.josseybass.com

Jossey-Bass books and products are available through most bookstores. To contact Jossey-Bass directly call our Customer Care Department within the U.S. at 800-956-7739, outside the U.S. at 317-572-3986, or fax 317-572-4002.

Wiley publishes in a variety of print and electronic formats and by print-on-demand. Some material included with standard print versions of this book may not be included in e-books or in print-on-demand. If this book refers to media such as a CD or DVD that is not included in the version you purchased, you may download this material at http://booksupport.wiley.com. For more information about Wiley products, visit www.wiley.com.

Library of Congress Cataloging-in-Publication Data

Elkington, John, date

The breakthrough challenge : 10 ways to connect today's profits with tomorrow's bottom line / John Elkington and Jochen Zeitz. — First edition.

pages cm

Includes index.

ISBN 978-1-118-53969-9 (hardback) —ISBN 978-1-118-92394-8 (pdf) — ISBN 978-1-118-92393-1 (epub)

1. Sustainable development. 2. Social responsibility of business. 3. Management— Environmental aspects. 4. Organizational change. I. Zeitz, Jochen. II. Title.

HC79.E5E4586 2014

658.4'08—dc23

2014007575

Printed in the United States of America

FIRST EDITION

HB Printing   10 9 8 7 6 5 4 3 2 1

Contents

Contents

To those who seek breakthrough change for a better world

Foreword

Sir Richard Branson

When I started Virgin several decades ago, I was excited to build businesses that made people's lives better. Holding true to this dream is an ongoing journey. We are constantly looking at ways to reinvent what we do to take better care of people and the planet, as well as make a profit. We've had some great successes, and we've also had our share of spectacular failures.

Over the last decade, we've seen a rapidly evolving movement of business leaders who want to create a *"Plan B for Business"* that connects the entrepreneurial drive to succeed with the needs of growing numbers of people and a planet under pressure. I've had the great pleasure of working with Jochen and John to take on this challenge. Both of them have been inspirations to me and to Virgin with the deep commitment they have to crafting a vision for this "Plan B" that shows that anything is possible and that business can and must play an exciting role in creating a new and better future for all. Over the last few years, we have joined forces with a great — and growing — group of partners to start The B Team, a strong coalition of global leaders who are catalyzing a better way of doing business, one that builds value while taking care of the well-being of people and planet. John Elkington, sometimes called the godfather of the modern sustainability movement, and Jochen Zeitz, co-chair of the B Team, sum up in *The Breakthrough Challenge* the B Team's mission: business is and must continue to be a force for good in this world, both in social and environmental terms. Ever the relentless optimist, I see that not as a frightening prospect, but as an amazing challenge. Success and sustainability are two sides of the same coin. Where the priorities of business and society align, everyone stands to gain. Better still, there are countless stories of entrepreneurial spirit and energies that help make the impossible possible.

Nothing is ever easy. Much of the business world continues to operate as if the financial crisis and all its resulting unrest never happened, but *The Breakthrough Challenge* has enormous potential to bring out the best in us — as all good challenges do. Leaders in all sectors, around the world, must recognize the need for a collective, concerted effort, and not shy away from setting bold targets.

Whether you are passionate about sustainable business, passionate about meeting stockholders' short-term profit expectations, or both, you know that our world is at a crossroads. As business leaders, entrepreneurs, investors, and advocates, the choice is ours: either we become part of the solution, or we will forever be seen as a major part of the problem. I choose the former, as do the members of The B Team, and we hope that you will, too.

Preface

Call it serendipity. We first met outside Geneva, at a small roundtable convened by Sir Richard Branson's foundation, Virgin Unite. The session explored early concepts for breakthrough capitalism[1] and for what ultimately would evolve into The B Team, a new grouping of CEOs and other leaders from the private, public, and citizen sectors. All those involved are dedicated to changing the rules not just of business but also of markets and, ultimately, of capitalism. The goal: a sustainable market economy. The proposed solution: Plan B, outlined in more detail in Chapter One.

The idea of pulling some of this together into a book came a couple of months later, as we explored converging interests. Back in 1994, John had coined the term "triple bottom line," and, in 1995, he came up with the linked term "people, planet, and profit."[2] As chance would have it, this book's year of publication marks the twentieth anniversary of the triple bottom line—and, many years later, the 3Ps would serve as The B Team's launch strapline as it began to evolve its Plan B agenda.

Jochen, meanwhile, had been the youngest-ever CEO of a German publicly listed company, Puma. His first book, *The Manager and the Monk*, was cowritten with Anselm Grün, a Benedictine monk and prolific author.[3] The book explored the overlap between prosperity, values, and sustainability from the viewpoints of both business and religion. Working with PwC and Trucost, Jochen had also pioneered the environmental profit and loss (EP&L) accounting approach at Puma and its Paris-based owner, the global group Kering. He saw the EP&L as the first step toward a full—and increasingly integrated—set of triple-bottom-line accounts. Ultimately, alongside an economic impact analysis, this would also include a social profit and loss (SP&L) element, with external stakeholders signaling that this is doable, although social accounting can be even more complex and political than environmental accounting.

Alongside the increasingly obvious challenges facing science, technology, and engineering, we need to transform economics and accounting to serve the transition to a sustainable future of an estimated nine to ten billion people later this century. This is what we mean by the Breakthrough Challenge, defined in more detail in our Introduction.

In this spirit, we tapped into the collective wisdom of The B Team leaders, of those who have helped to shape the B Team agenda, and of around a hundred other leaders and change agents. Soon we had a global conversation on our hands. Our interviewees ran the gamut from Justin Welby, the then newly appointed archbishop of Canterbury and himself a former businessman, to Zhang Yue, one of the most successful industrialists in China, the world's most successful (if still profoundly illiberal) Communist economy.

Our hope is that The B Team and its evolving Plan B agenda, whatever reverses they may suffer along the way, will help drive and shape the next wave of change. With such a fast-paced entrepreneurial initiative, it is inevitable that The B Team agenda will evolve considerably, with new priority areas being added as new members join. But this is our best shot at capturing the state of play at one of the most exciting ventures either of us has been involved in to date.

We hope you find the book both provocative and useful. The conversations continue to build as The B Team defines the concrete actions it plans to pursue, so please join us. Let's accept and tackle the Breakthrough Challenge together.

April 2014

John Elkington
Jochen Zeitz

The Breakthrough Challenge

Introduction

Profit from Tomorrow's Bottom Line

Much of the world has entered one of those rare epochal periods when business, markets, and even capitalism itself face a succession of breakdowns.[1] Political, economic, and societal failures are causing many of us to lose confidence in the old order. Too often, our politicians and governments, desperate to safeguard their own interests and protect their electoral prospects, lack the will to make the hard decisions needed to create a new order that works for all.

As confidence in the old world order erodes, those with an eye to the future are looking for radically different solutions. In the process, a growing number of business leaders are beginning to notice innovations they had previously ignored. They also are starting to consider new ways to perform not only against today's measures of success but also against tomorrow's bottom line. Where a few breakthrough leaders currently work to map out the new landscapes of risk and opportunity, the coming years will see increasing numbers of breakthrough leaders, businesses, and industries pushing way beyond today's change-as-usual strategies.

This is the Breakthrough Challenge. It requires us to coevolve a shared vision of a radically better future—and to work out new ways to measure and incentivize progress. The business breakthrough that will make this possible is tomorrow's bottom line, and as it evolves, it must become a North Star for business leaders and investors determined to future-proof their assets and organizations.

Tomorrow's bottom line may still be emergent, but we can already detect an outline and some key features. The focus will vary across different geographies, sectors, and ownership structures, but at its heart will be a new appreciation of longer-term thinking, strategy, and investment. It will place a higher value on ambition and stretch targets. Its evolution will be powered by radically greater market transparency. It will track novel forms of capital and value, using numbers and algorithms that would seem alien to most of today's financial analysts and CFOs. It will be integrated in new ways, linking to wider metrics on the health and well-being of individuals, communities, and ecosystems. It will favor businesses that learn from nature and play into the emerging circular economy. Critically, it also will be supported by a broadening range of professions and service industries that seek to level the market playing field—upward.

Our focus can no longer be on a single, financial bottom line. Future success—lasting success—will mean much more than posting positive quarterly earnings or boosting stock prices by a penny a share. In a world that is increasingly intertwined and interdependent, we must consider people and the planet as well as profits.

We must build the foundations of tomorrow's prosperity by expanding the focus of accounting and reporting from *financial* and *manufactured* forms of capital (for example, infrastructures, buildings, and equipment) to embrace other forms, including *intellectual* (intellectual property, patents, tacit knowledge, and intangible assets like brands), *human* (people's competencies, capabilities, and experience), *social* (shared norms, common values, key stakeholder relationships, and an organization's social license to operate), and *natural* (air, water, land, minerals, forests, biodiversity, and wider ecosystem health) forms.

The consequences are likely to be as profound as those triggered by the development of new scientific and political paradigms during the Enlightenment or the spread of fossil-fuel-consuming technologies during the Industrial Revolution or the lightning-quick changes that marked the dawn of the Internet age. As a result, the quest is now on for new mind-sets, new technologies, new business and economic models, and new lifestyles and cultures.

Increasingly, it will be a question of breakdown or breakthrough. Breakthrough leaders — and increasingly their organizations — are coming to understand the need for new levels of ambition, innovation, and enterprise. They also acknowledge that it is now up to business to accept the challenge.

o Business Must Take the Lead

Faced with a perfect storm involving globalization, the increasing power of multinational corporations, and the impact of the prolonged economic downturn, most governments have struggled to keep up with events — let alone get out ahead of them. In this context, a growing number of CEOs and other business leaders publicly acknowledge that our economies and societies face new and increasingly systemic challenges. They conclude that there are material business implications and that in the absence of effective government action, business has no option but to take the lead.

They do not do this because they want no (or less) government, but because they see political leaders — and many parts of the public sector — trapped in something of a time warp. These business leaders no longer simply talk about cleaning up their own operations and supply chains. They also stress the need to change key aspects of the very capitalist system of which they have been among the main beneficiaries. They want—and they increasingly will insist on—new forms of politics and government that are better adapted for the twenty-first century.

Feike Sijbesma is CEO and chairman of the managing board at Royal DSM. Royal DSM started out as Dutch State Mines, an extractive and coal-to-chemicals operation, then morphed into an industrial chemicals producer and then increasingly into a global science-based company active in health, nutrition, and materials. Sijbesma is among the leaders who have concluded that our economic and societal systems are no longer fit for purpose.

"When the richest quarter of the world's population uses about half of our global resources—and takes the liberty to produce almost half of the global waste—while another third lives in poverty," he says, "it is clear that our economic and societal systems are failing us. And that is even before we consider how our planet needs to accommodate nine billion mostly urbanized and aging people, and the enormous pressure we see on our climate and environmental systems. Add in the rapidly growing middle class in China, India, and elsewhere who also want their share, and it is easy to see that our current path is unsustainable."

Sijbesma believes—as we do—that urgent global challenges now call for a radical overhaul of the economic system. He argues for the need to strike a new balance in which societal, ecological, and economic value creation are seen as three equal and complementary goals for business.

Doug Miller, founder and chairman of the global polling firm GlobeScan, notes that governments are failing when it comes to driving this sort of change. He concludes that business-led solutions now represent the only realistic option when it comes to providing a path toward new measures of value creation that look well beyond the financial numbers. Drawing on his firm's polling of tens of thousands of experts and citizens in scores of countries, he reports that "stakeholders and experts alike are beginning to see business-led solutions as pretty much all we've got to work with, in the absence of government and of really effective NGOs."

When it comes to corporate board and C-suite engagement, Miller concludes that the business case is still often too weak to engage top teams hemmed in by such factors as investor insistence on quarterly reporting and earnings guidance. "Our hope has to be in next-generation leaders, with significant progress now just a promotion away," Miller concludes. This is a huge opportunity for tomorrow's leaders now moving into the global C-suite. They must lead the way in both providing solutions and encouraging their colleagues to embrace the Breakthrough Challenge.

o Introducing The B Team

It is this agenda — this kind of change — that the founders of The B Team champion. The B Team is a nonprofit initiative formed by a group of global business leaders to work toward a future in which the purpose of business is to be a driving force for social, environmental, and economic benefit and change. They have come together as concerned global citizens, not just as representatives of their companies or sectors. Simply stated, they aim to contribute to changing the rules of the market game.

Their mission is to deliver a "Plan B" that places people and the planet at least equally alongside profit.[2] "Plan A," they conclude, in which "companies have been driven by the profit motive alone — is no longer acceptable."[3] There is no Planet B, as B team cofounder Sir Richard Branson insists. However, drawing on the priorities of the founding CEOs and of hundreds of other leaders around the world, there is now an evolving Plan B.[4]

The members of The B Team include leaders straddling many different sectors around the world.[5] Sir Richard Branson and Jochen Zeitz, coauthor of this book, cofounded the organization and serve as cochairs. Leaders in the first round of members were:[6]

Shari Arison (owner, Arison Group, Israel)

Kathy Calvin (president and chief executive, UN Foundation)

Arianna Huffington (president and editor-in-chief, the Huffington Post Media Group, USA)

Dr. Mo Ibrahim (founder of Celtel; chair, Mo Ibrahim Foundation, Sudan-U.K.)

Guilherme Leal (cofounder and board member, Natura; founder, Instituto Arapyaú, Brazil)

Strive Masiyiwa (founder and chairman, Econet Wireless, Zimbabwe/South Africa)

Blake Mycoskie (founder and chief shoe giver, TOMS, USA)

Dr. Ngozi Okonjo-Iweala (coordinating minister of the economy and minister of finance, Nigeria)

François-Henri Pinault (chairman and CEO, Kering, France)

Paul Polman (CEO, Unilever, the Netherlands)

Ratan Tata (chairman emeritus, Tata Sons, India)

Muhammad Yunus (Nobel Prize–winning founder of Grameen Bank, Bangladesh)

Zhang Yue (chairman and founder, Broad Group, China)

Two honorary members also joined in the first round: Gro Harlem Brundtland (former prime minister of Norway) and Mary Robinson (former president of Ireland).

These leaders think and act differently — and they use different measures of success. "For several years now, all our business and philanthropic entities have been implementing long-term visions and instilling values," reports Shari Arison. "And now I can say that we're proving that *doing good is good business*. It's a whole new way of doing business that many companies are waking up to."[7]

Such people often report having had a wake-up moment. Blake Mycoskie of TOMS recalls being shocked to see shoeless children in Argentina in 2006.

> That really was the ah-ha moment for me. Most people look at problems in the third world and one word comes to mind: charity. But for me the word entrepreneurship came to mind. And that's why I started TOMS as a for-profit business with our One for One model. I knew if we could get people to buy our shoes, and continue to buy our shoes, that we could sustain the giving and that would solve the issue that I saw in Argentina. Five years later, we launched the second One for One: TOMS Eyewear, helping to provide sight to those in need around the world. To date, TOMS has given over ten million pairs of new shoes to children in need and has helped to restore 175,000 people's vision around the world.[8]

Everyone involved in The B Team is committed to working toward long-term, breakthrough solutions that will open up new pathways to more sustainable, more equitable societies and economies. As Gro Harlem Brundtland notes, "the process of reinvention must include private actors, businesses, and civil society, encouraging them all to take a long-term view."

In the simplest terms, a series of complex challenges boils down to four commitments that leaders must make. First, the leaders aim to reduce harm to the planet—and to support its restoration. Second, they pledge to make the well-being of people a priority. Third, they are committed to ensuring good governance and transparency. Fourth, they are collaborating to accelerate better ways of doing business—stressing that a key part of this will involve working with governments to ensure fair and transparent tax systems, alongside new types of incentives designed to promote better outcomes for people and the planet.

B Team member Zhang Yue, founder and chairman of Broad Group, is an example of these commitments in action. He founded his business with just $3,000 in 1988. Since then he has obtained over one hundred patents for his inventions, ranging from the pressure-free hot water boiler in 1989 to a factory-made sustainable building twenty years later, and is known for working at an ultra-rapid pace, including building a fifteen-story hotel in just fifteen days. In 2011, Zhang was awarded the UN Champions of the Earth award; the citation noted that he had "become one of the most outspoken voices on the environment in China, advocating, among other things, for tighter government regulations on insulation and building standards and for the decentralization of power plants."[9]

We recognize that what The B Team proposes will be a challenge to — in some cases even taken as an affront by — some of our colleagues and competitors. We understand that embracing this kind of change — both in thought and action — can be intimidating. But experience suggests that together, over time, we can move toward radically better ways of doing business. What seems impossible today can seem possible — even inevitable — tomorrow.

Rather than simply protesting the various ways in which the current order is undermining the future, The B Team is committed to catalyzing the emergence of a new economic order. Working with a global community of advisers and partners, The B Team leaders focus on execution and action, catalyzing and amplifying others' efforts by undertaking specific global challenges where their collective voice can make a difference. In picking challenges to tackle, The B Team aims to ensure that the challenges it accepts pass through all — or most — of the following five "decision gates":

- Will this proposed solution remove a critical roadblock or create enabling conditions to ensure that business works significantly better for people and the planet as well as profit?

- Will the solution lead to an entirely new expectation, model, ideology, or system for how business is done?
- Are the various proposed solutions to a particular challenge scalable? Is there existing work that the team can accelerate to cause greater impact at a faster rate without duplication?
- Is this a challenge—and are these solutions—that are best advanced by business? Or would it be more appropriate for some other entity?
- Is this challenge a good fit for The B Team, and does it fill an important gap in the world (that is, does it ultimately serve to accomplish Plan B)?

To help focus its efforts, The B Team has identified four overarching challenges: the future bottom line, the future of incentives, the future of leadership, and the future of investment. Here's what we mean by each of them:

- **The future bottom line.** During the past century, most publicly listed companies have increasingly focused on the single objective of profit maximization, often driving short-term financial gains at a long-term cost to people and the planet. Business has not accounted for the true cost of its activities when it comes to negative impacts on individuals, society, and the environment. The bottom-line performance reported to investors, therefore, does not reflect the true health and status of a given business. The B Team, by contrast, strives to accelerate the move away from single-minded financial short-termism toward a greater focus on the long term, and aims to expand corporate accountability beyond financial gains to include both positive and negative contributions to the economy, society, and the environment. (See Chapters Three and Four.)

- **The future of incentives.** Current global regulatory frameworks rarely support the transition of markets and business models toward what we would understand as tomorrow's bottom line. There are too few positive incentives and too many perverse ones. So The B Team is working with partners to develop new corporate and employee incentive structures. It also aims to identify and map both positive and harmful subsidies, helping build business support for incentives that maximize economic, social, and environmental benefit and dividends. (See Chapter Six.)

- **The future of leadership.** Because the current mind-set of competing and consuming primarily for financial gain is unsustainable, business leaders must work together to build the new foundations for tomorrow's growth. Focusing on the need to redefine what it means to be a good leader in business, The B Team aims to accelerate a new kind of inclusive leadership underpinned by a moral compass of being fair, honest, positive, and creative.[10] This approach is founded on cooperation and aims to generate long-term value for society, the economy, and the environment. Working with others, we will highlight and celebrate those who are leading the way and helping nurture a new generation of business leaders. (See Chapters Eight and Ten.)

- **The future of investment.** Today's capital largely flows to companies and businesses that focus obsessively on profit. In contrast, The B Team concludes that it is time to steer a much greater proportion of future investment into activities creating new blends of economic, social, and environmental value, what Jed Emerson has dubbed "blended value." We cover the financial world in several chapters, but particularly in Chapters Three, Four, and Ten and in our Conclusion.

Reaching these goals will require leaders to contribute their fair share, work toward climate justice, respect planetary boundaries, and improve governance and transparency wherever they operate. These aspirations, decision gates, and challenges are a lot to take in, but this level of change is rarely easy. There is no getting around the fact that delivering the kind of systemic change now needed will require breakthrough thinking from breakthrough leaders to help push us to — and beyond — the tipping point.

Ten Steps to Breakthrough

The B Team concludes that leaders both in business and other sectors will need to undertake at least ten key steps in order to respond to the Breakthrough Challenge in time and in good order:

- Adopt the right aspirations
- Create new corporate structures
- Apply true accounting principles
- Calculate true returns
- Embrace well-being
- Level the playing field
- Pursue full transparency
- Redefine education
- Learn from nature's model
- Keep the long run in mind

Adopt the Right Aspirations

Talk to some senior business leaders who have tried to push beyond change-as-usual strategies, and their deep frustration with the pace of progress is clear. Sir Mark Moody-Stuart, former CEO of Shell, former chairman at Anglo-American, and now on the board of Saudi Aramco, is just one of the leaders who have been pushing for breakthrough change. What we need now, he insists, is transformation. He notes that we are seeing the dawn of what geologists (of which he is one) call the Anthropocene. "We are having unusual impact as a species, and it will have consequences," he says. He also warns that at least some pioneering business leaders have found supporting the sustainability agenda grueling. "Leading CEOs are battle-weary," he explains. "Shell, for example, has been working on climate change for almost twenty years—and not much has happened."

Although the twin concepts of corporate citizenship and corporate social responsibility have gained traction in recent decades, they have been increasingly criticized as not ambitious enough. They also have been challenged on the basis that those who champion such concepts are often remote from the board and C-suite world where the key priorities are set and real decisions are made, that they fail to shape a company's business model, that their initiatives too easily degenerate into public relations, that they rarely address systemic challenges, and that often they are difficult to replicate and scale.

It is striking, for example, that 81 percent of 766 CEOs polled a few years back were convinced that they had already "embedded" sustainability into their organizations.[11] What they meant, it seems, was that they were already engaging a wider range of stakeholders, producing nonfinancial reports, and, perhaps, considering appointing a chief sustainability officer. What they were not thinking of was the need to drive systemic change.

By contrast, the leaders who are backing The B Team and its Plan B agenda insist that the time has come for breakthrough thinking. It is time, they say, to adopt the right aspirations, moving well beyond current approaches to corporate citizenship and corporate social responsibility. We'll look at these new aspirations and what they mean for tomorrow's business leaders in Chapter One.

Create New Corporate Structures

It is time to accelerate the evolution and adoption of new corporate structures. In many cases, this will require changing ownership patterns, which is one of the toughest challenges business leaders are likely to face.

We need to think of business in very different ways. For example, B Team member and Nobel Peace Prize winner Muhammad Yunus promotes what he dubs "social business." A social business is "a nondividend company created to solve a social problem. Like an NGO, it has a social mission, but like a business, it generates its own revenues both to cover its costs and to produce a surplus. While investors may recoup their investment, all further profits are reinvested into the same or other social businesses," he explains.[12]

A different approach, and one that is being adopted by a growing number of for-profit, social-mission businesses, involves a business registering as a "benefit corporation" (or B Corp). This approach offers an integrated pathway that aligns businesses with social and environmental interests. B Corp certification requires a corporate mission that encompasses social and environmental impact, a governance structure that supports that mission and measurement, and transparency of social and environmental impact using comparable yardsticks. Among other things, B Corps are challenged to keep the bar high, to scale as quickly as possible, and to maintain effective transparency.

Social businesses and B Corps are just two of the new forms of corporate structure and ownership that will influence the future shape of business. Indeed, there are many alternatives to the publicly listed corporations that dominate today's media. Cooperatives, family-owned businesses, state-owned enterprises, and other ownership formats already make up a large part of the global economy—a proportion that is likely to grow significantly in the coming years. We must get much better at tracking, engaging, and influencing these very different styles of business. We'll look at some of these new corporate forms in Chapter Two.

Apply True Accounting Principles

Unlikely as it may seem, some accountants are adopting the role of market transformers. Anyone familiar with the evolution of accounting, including double-entry bookkeeping, knows what an extraordinary achievement financial accounting is—and how well, overall, it has served our economies. Recent decades, however, have seen a dawning realization that we should track not just one bottom line, with one profit and loss statement, but several—spanning multiple forms of capital and value. Otherwise, how can you know that what you are doing is the right thing beyond your conventionally defined financial bottom line?

Companies of every sort must now prepare for tomorrow's market and governance imperatives. Much attention is currently focused on the environmental dimensions of the challenge. Breakthrough organizations must work out ways to "demonstrate how natural capital accounting can be used by companies to assess natural capital risk and opportunity embedded within their operations and supply chains," explains Richard Mattison, chief executive of Trucost, an organization that, as we will see, operates at the cutting edge of multidimensional accounting. The ethical, social, and governance aspects of business also need to be tracked, evaluated, and reported.

Ultimately, success in this critically important area will depend on the outcomes of experiments under way in such areas as environmental profit and loss (EP&L), social profit and loss (SP&L), and new forms of integrated accounting and reporting. We'll look at progress in terms of what The B Team calls "true accounting" principles in Chapter Three.

Calculate True Returns

In addition to advancing new (and truer) accounting principles, The B Team aims to ensure that the conditions exist for finance to flow in a relevant and timely way toward ventures and initiatives that aim to perform in terms of the triple-bottom-line agenda of people, planet, and profit.

This will be a tall order. Eventually, if enough capital is to be injected into conscious, regenerative, and sustainable forms of capitalism, business leaders will need to help transform the master discipline of economics itself. As the true cost of business activities is increasingly factored in, it is inevitable that increasing numbers of investors will be left with what are known as "stranded assets." These are financial assets that have become obsolete in some way; as a consequence, they are no longer able to generate a financial return, and so must be recorded on the balance sheet as an actual or potential loss.

Calculating the true cost of such issues as global warming will be an imperative for tomorrow's breakthrough organizations. Fundamentally, we need a radical reimagining and reinventing of the very notion of capitalism. We'll look in Chapter Four at how this might happen.

Embrace Well-Being

The business world must become a powerful driver of human, social, and planetary well-being. Terms like "holistic well-being" may seem unconnected with financial well-being or corporate well-being, but they are powerfully linked—and will become even more so over time.

At its best, the well-being approach creates social value by helping evolve business models, providing employee welfare, protecting safety and health, and promoting citizen engagement and human rights. A growing body of researchers has looked closely at well-being in recent years, at the levels of individuals, communities, and even nations, including efforts to measure and put a value on happiness. For example, there is a Happy Planet Index, which aims to measure the extent to which countries deliver long, happy, sustainable lives for their citizens.[13] Elsewhere, there are plans to establish gross national happiness alongside more traditional measures like gross national product.

Measuring happiness and well-being may seem a little too intangible for business leaders who have long been taught and incentivized to focus on a narrower range of "hard" numbers. However, tomorrow's leaders, at least those who fully embrace the Breakthrough Challenge, will assume from the very outset that well-being is a key to ultimate business success. We'll look at this in greater detail in Chapter Five.

Level the Playing Field

Business leaders often use "level playing field" arguments to push for the addition, dilution, or abandonment of proposed new government rules. Routinely, they—and their industry federations—have prioritized self-interest and short-term outcomes over outcomes that are vital for the longer-term health of the economies and societies they are in business to serve.

Now the focus must shift to the question of how to tilt market playing fields toward more sustainable outcomes—for all (or at least most) players. As part of this transition, The B Team encourages the progressive—and accelerating—removal of subsidies or incentives for practices that are destructive to people and the planet. Wherever you look, the world is rife with rules, subsidies, and incentives that may benefit particular companies, sectors, or economies but put at risk numerous people and, in some cases, the entire planet.

There's not much that The B Team leaders can do on their own to head off all risks here, but a challenge exists that they see as increasingly problematic—and where they now intend to use their influence and political leverage. Of key interest is the contentious area of ill-considered or obsolete government subsidies, particularly so-called perverse subsidies. These distort the global economy by, for example, favoring the exploitation of climate-destabilizing fossil fuels, destructive overfishing, or the overconsumption of water and other resources, while also discouraging the scaling of sustainable business models.

Less visible, but often equally pernicious, is the issue of corruption, tackled by what is sometimes called "anticorruption." Excused in many parts of the world as "part of our culture" or "the way things have always been done around here," bribery and corruption skew decision making toward more personal and tribal outcomes. They have a corrosive effect on the capacity for long-term thinking. Too often, they result in market distortions on an epic scale.

Unsurprisingly, many business leaders feel that it is beyond them to find ways to tackle such market distortions, especially when governments are often heavily involved in maintaining the skewed status quo. The work of business-led NGOs like Transparency International is showing the way forward to cleaner business, cleaner markets, and, above all, cleaner governments.

In the same spirit, tomorrow's breakthrough businesses will seek ways to level the playing field for all players, regardless of affiliation, sector, or location. Tomorrow's leaders will work together to advance regulations that punish problematic, unsustainable activities. This calls for some profound rethinking, and in Chapter Six we'll look at how this might be done.

Pursue Full Transparency

Transparency has long been a business issue. In competitive markets, companies routinely trade off the need for transparency to satisfy investors and other stakeholders with the need for stealth to protect new thinking and intellectual property. Unfortunately, there are those who pursue secrecy for different reasons. The debacle with Enron and Arthur Andersen in 2001 was the present century's first clear demonstration of the perils of stealth, and since then, much discussion and many regulations have tried to boost market transparency. The trouble is that many high-profile organizations talk a good game in this area without yet being transparent in any meaningful way.

Tomorrow's breakthrough organizations and sectors will find it imperative to embrace unprecedented levels of transparency. Publicly listed, high-profile, big-brand businesses will increasingly operate in a "CAT scan" environment, where the outside world will be able to look deeply into everything, from where their materials and ingredients come from, to the energy costs associated with shipping products, to the level of well-being of their employees, to their lobbying positions on key issues.

Making sense of this will require new types of accounting and reporting, with the rapidly emerging fields of sustainability reporting and integrated reporting providing crucial tools to inform choices and decisions. Over time, accounting methods like the EP&L and the SP&L also promise to create information allowing top teams, employees, clients, customers, joint venture partners, suppliers, and other key stakeholders to gain a deeper understanding of the organizations they work for, buy from, or invest in.

Ultimately, the pursuit of real—and sometimes radical—transparency will require organizations to report on their contributions to the emerging "circular economy," which aims progressively to decouple wealth and welfare from the consumption of natural resources. A key feature of this new approach will be to assign a realistic value to natural capital, taking into account the depreciation of resources and the loss of biodiversity as well as the linked impacts on other forms of capital. Key tools in determining how much room we have to maneuver are emerging in such areas as ecological and social "footprinting." Such approaches acknowledge that we live on a small planet, with burgeoning human populations straddling the extremes of the wealth divide, and that we urgently need to reboot our mind-sets, values, and institutions so that they are fit for the future.

Uncomfortable or not, transparency will be the sine qua non of progress. One day, perhaps, every product—from a box of cereal to a sewage system—will be able to tell us its life story and report on its ongoing performance against local, industry, or global benchmarks. In the meantime, we must find new, more powerful ways to keep a watchful eye on producers and their supply chains. We'll dig deeper into this issue in Chapter Seven.

Redefine Education

A truly sustainable future will require an increasingly educated, informed, and active citizenry. Radical transparency will do much to help educate people across the planet about the challenges we all face and the responses of key organizations and institutions. The B Team also wants to help ensure that the next generation is taught and inspired to understand that the purpose of business is to be a driving force for social and environmental benefit, not just for financial gain. Further, pretty much all the founding group of The B Team CEOs flag youth opportunity, unemployment, and education as critical challenges and necessary vectors of change.

Changing what and how universities and business schools teach will be part of the answer, of course, but the scale of the challenge also demands that education break out of the classroom. Happily, that is already happening, with social enterprises like the Khan Academy and Coursera offering open access to rapidly growing bodies of educational resources that once would have remained locked up inside educational institutions. Organizations around the world are embracing new forms of education and training, which will be crucial as we begin to tackle the huge behavioral and cultural challenges that loom ahead.

Among other things, these new forms of education necessitate a rethinking of business schools in general and of MBA programs in particular. Although there is no shortage of business schools nor of MBA students, this particular advanced degree has, at least in some circles, lost some of its luster. No longer is gaining an MBA from a top school a guaranteed path to business success. Smart business leaders recognize that recruiting top talent often means looking beyond traditional sources to find individuals who are well versed in the new skills needed to run businesses in tomorrow's very different market conditions — regardless of what school they earned their degree from, or indeed whether they have a business degree at all.

Tomorrow's breakthrough leaders and organizations will understand that they must rethink education and redefine the ways in which they recruit and retain top talent. Among other things, that will mean taking a much deeper look at experiential learning, study tours, and learning journeys. It will also mean that business must exert more pressure on the world of B-schools and universities to ensure that they inspire and teach their students how to value and pursue social, environmental, and financial benefit. We'll look at all of this in Chapter Eight.

Learn from Nature's Model

Our education systems aren't the only sources of learning and insight. Nature has been evolving solutions to complex challenges for billions of years. Realizing this, a growing number of designers and engineers are looking to the natural world for breakthrough ideas about how business can become more conscious, responsible, sustainable, and regenerative. The B Team aims to ensure that instead of depleting and polluting natural resources, business increasingly works with — not against — the grain of nature.

The emerging discipline of biomimicry, led by such pioneers as Janine Benyus of the Biomimicry 3.8 Institute, is having a growing impact on thinking, design, and engineering. The central idea is to use natural models as a guide for evolving an ever-wider spectrum of materials, products, processes, communities, cities, and even entire economies.

This is set to be a rich area of innovation, offering powerful clues as to where the economy will head next. As the relevant information resources are built into the latest computer-aided design programs and algorithms, business leaders will have at their disposal a rich supply of innovative ideas for breakthrough products and services. We'll explore where that might take us in Chapter Nine.

Keep the Long Run in Mind

It's time for a reality check. Even with the best will in the world, little of what we have outlined here will happen or work unless we can seriously stretch our collective time horizons. So The B Team leaders aim to help ensure that business horizons are considerably extended from the short, quarterly focus of today to the significantly longer-term horizons of tomorrow's markets.

No one doubts that a short-term focus is sometime necessary. However, the Great Recession violently truncated many people's timescales, aggravating the short-termism of many businesses as they battled for survival and sought to conserve (rather than invest) their funds in times of considerable uncertainty.

On the upside, the leaders spotlighted later in the book recognize that there are now powerful reasons to embrace longer-term thinking. At a time when the competitive pressure is increasing from forward-thinking China, short-termism will likely prove dangerous to those businesses and economies that keep their eyes down.

At the same time, as our economies shift and change, there will be a growing number of opportunities to tap into the aspirations and expertise of new generations of leaders and talented people whose training and education have convinced them that at a time when science and technology are changing everything — at historically unparalleled speeds — we are headed into what some people dub a new normal. Individuals, businesses, and governments are not simply more connected than ever before, but now need to form new "ecosystems of change" if they are to succeed in tackling the Breakthrough Challenge.

That said, real-time information, minute-by-minute headlines, and nanosecond trading can make it much more difficult for many executives to look beyond quarterly earnings to longer-term risks and opportunities. It will take much to change that market reality, but history suggests that it is during times like these that leaders and ventures can succeed in breaking through with new thinking, technologies, and business models, creating value in unprecedented ways. We'll look more closely at the time dimension in Chapter Ten.

o Breaking Through Requires System Change

Each of the ten principles of Plan B speaks to the increasingly urgent task of system change. Business leaders determined to steer their organizations toward true wealth creation will need to explore and embrace these principles, apply them diligently, and, crucially, champion them as a new breed of change agents. Leaders who do so will be well on their way to building the breakthrough corporations and organizations that will powerfully shape tomorrow's new normal.

Tomorrow's bottom line will measure progress toward a world in which breakthrough leaders and organizations lead the way. This will be a long journey, full of surprises and reverses. Like all journeys, however, it must start with that first, critical step: adopting the right aspirations, which is where we turn next.

1

Adopt the Right Aspirations

"We are the leaders we have been waiting for," insisted a McKinsey & Company director in a recent report viewing California's future through a triple-bottom-line lens.[1]

That remains to be seen, but both he and the other five hundred or so economic leaders who attended the 2013 California Economic Summit, on which that report was based, understand that nowadays there is not just one California, but at least two: one coastal and fairly wealthy, one inland and poorer. As elsewhere around the globe, there are worlds of haves and of have-nots. Now, for better or worse, like it or not, transformational change is coming. "Our job as leaders," explained Gavin Newsom, lieutenant-governor of California and former mayor of San Francisco, "is to create the right conditions where success is irresistible."

Easier said than done. However, as we work toward a new economic order, breakthrough leaders are at last signaling that the old order is broken — unsustainable. Wherever and however their journeys started, they bring new thinking and new aspirations that push well beyond current profitability calculations to blaze a new path toward solutions that also serve the wider interests of people and the planet. They aim uncomfortably high — and expect their colleagues, their contractors, and even their competitors to follow suit.

○ Ten Aspirations for Breakthrough Leadership

The B Team underscores the need to stretch our aspirations and ambitions. Indeed, ambition is at the very heart of Plan B. During a meeting in late 2013, The B Team leaders outlined ten aspirations for breakthrough leadership:

- Aim to do the apparently impossible.
- Hold yourself accountable to all stakeholders, including future generations.
- Take the lead. Don't count on governments and NGOs to act first.
- Be truly ambitious across the entire people-planet-profit agenda.
- Create partnerships that have the potential to become much more than the sum of their parts.
- Be bold, but at the same time seek simple, practical solutions that companies can share.
- Redefine what successful businesses and success in business look like, understanding that businesses can still make money while having strong ethical values and a positive impact on both people and the planet.
- Help catalyze new social and political movements, aggregating the various submovements into a "movement of movements," and help push them past a tipping point toward achieving the Plan B objectives.
- Provide an authoritative voice with a compelling, persuasive narrative that sketches the future we must now create.
- Engage and help mobilize people, particularly young people — whose future this will be.

Only if great numbers of business leaders take responsibility in this way are the Plan B goals achievable. In simple terms, The B Team concludes that breakthrough leaders, across the global economy, must become effective catalysts for radically better ways of doing business. Business clearly cannot make these changes on its own: political leaders, governments, and the public sector also will be crucial in designing and rolling out the new order. When businesses adopt these aspirations in the right way and at the right time, however, they can help build the critical mass needed to move all leaders toward breakthrough thinking, solutions, and outcomes.

Aim to Do the Apparently Impossible

Too often, leaders become entrenched in the art of the possible, forgetting to look beyond to the apparently out of the question. When everything is running smoothly, it's easy to know what is expected, and the "right" answers are available more or less off the shelf. However, in times of Schumpeterian creative destruction—as we are experiencing today—incumbent industries stumble, and new breeds of insurgent come to the fore, just as they did in the era of Thomas Edison and Henry Ford. Just as they are doing today with the likes of Jeff Bezos, Richard Branson, Larry Page and Sergei Brin, Elon Musk, Craig Venter, and Zhang Yue. (Zhang is also a member of The B Team and a leading Chinese businessman known for making more sustainable air-conditioning systems and low-impact skyscrapers, among other things.)

Such innovators are motivated by the same sort of thinking that drives people like Peter Diamandis and his extraordinary X Prize Foundation, which awards prizes for innovators and entrepreneurs who aim to solve the world's most pressing problems and whose inspiring motto is "Making the Impossible Possible."

The inventors, innovators, entrepreneurs, and investors we remember best include those who at first got it spectacularly wrong and then, often after painful lessons along the way, got it spectacularly right. These pioneers were not afraid to tackle apparently impossible challenges. Imagine a world in which these risk takers opted for the status quo, where the Wright Brothers chose not to pursue their dreams of manned flight or where Alexander Graham Bell dismissed the telephone out of hand.

Breakthrough leaders know what they must do, or are determined to explore and find out along the way. Like Jeff Bezos and Steve Jobs, they often erupt from unrelated areas, usually because the old "right" solutions—some of which were the breakthroughs of their day—aren't the right answers now. Think of PayPal cofounder Elon Musk, who went on to disrupt three industries in succession: the auto world with Tesla, the energy world with SolarCity, and the space business with SpaceX. In picking him as its Businessperson of the Year in 2013, *Fortune* magazine noted that "Musk's creations have already made him tremendously wealthy—Bloomberg Wealth says he is worth $7.7 billion—but it is his audacity and tenacity that make him *Fortune's* Businessperson of the Year."[2]

Audacity and tenacity are going to be necessary conditions for true long-term sustainability. No matter where they come from or what industry they are involved in, breakthrough leaders understand that they cannot leave transformative change to others. They know that it is they who must innovate, invent, and iterate. They understand that there isn't time to wait for someone else to take responsibility for the future, and two of the most important questions they must ask are "If not us, who?" and "If not now, when?"

Hold Yourself Accountable

Breakthrough leaders understand that the world is increasingly interdependent. No longer can businesses focus solely on the traditional bottom line alone or on the interests and demands of majority shareholders. Instead, these leaders are concluding that they must hold themselves accountable to all relevant stakeholders, including future generations.

Taking responsibility means more than simply issuing a promissory note — or press release — pledging that your organization is going to be more transparent or that it will institute a new program to encourage simultaneous financial, social, and environmental progress and wider well-being. Breakthrough leaders know that they must challenge everyone throughout their organizations to adopt actions that drive toward the new targets and measures of accountability and performance. To lead effectively, they must identify the weaknesses not only of their business model and colleagues but also of their own mind-sets, experience, and skill sets.

They understand that they must work to change the rules of the game, where the current rules incentivize the wrong outcomes. A key part of this agenda involves lobbying for more effective governments. This is an area where business and many civil society organizations can now find new forms of common ground.

Most of The B Team leaders would agree with Greenpeace's international director, Kumi Naidoo, when he says, "Without clear rules and effective governments, too many companies will continue to free-ride society." It is easy to see why this is the case. As Naidoo puts it, businesses, on average, "would lose forty-one cents for every dollar in earnings if they were made to pay the full environmental costs of their operations." We can argue about the numbers, but it is clear that internalizing these sorts of externalities will be acutely painful for many incumbent industries.

Take the Lead

It can be brutally tough to be the first one to make a move in a competitive arena, especially when it comes to the kind of systemic changes that The B Team calls for. All too often, incumbent businesses expect others to pioneer new paths and look to governments to proffer a green light, whether through new regulations or new incentives. In uncertain times, however, politicians and governments often play for safety. They try to restore the status quo, rather than helping roll out what we might call the "future quo."[3] They use lobbying from those industries vested in the old order as an alibi for inaction. In doing so, they fail to recognize that inaction is itself a form of action: their efforts to shore up the old order serve to block or slow the efforts of those investing in the new order.

Similarly, many businesses still look to NGOs to lead the way, often finding that it's easier to follow or copy or be inspired by trailblazing leaders and organizations. However, business is uniquely equipped with the tools and resources to make a real difference. Business leaders must learn how to guide and work with NGOs, not the other way around. "Corporations potentially bring much more to the table than cash, including their business expertise, supply chains, marketing capabilities, and employee engagement," stresses Kathy Calvin, member of The B Team and CEO of the UN Foundation. "The nonprofit sector, particularly in international development, must learn to work with the business sector in a fully integrated manner—and not think of companies just as financial donors."

The B Team encourages all business leaders to do what they are meant to do: think hard, rethink where necessary, and lead. Leaders make a fundamental mistake if they wait for others to act. Instead, they must take the plunge, helping others do likewise and, in particular, encouraging politicians and policymakers to follow suit, putting their own (and potentially formidable) shoulders to the wheel of change.

Be Truly Ambitious

When it comes to adopting the right aspirations, true leaders must help change the rules of the game right across the people-planet-profit agenda. Although The B Team leaders understand that the only way to eat the metaphorical elephant is one bite at a time, they also understand that the world can't just sit back and wait for the kind of systemic change needed to adapt our mind-sets and mental models to be fit for a future world straining at the seams with a predicted population of over nine billion people by midcentury.

Among those who are most ambitious are the "Zeronauts"—innovators, change agents, and policymakers working to drive societal ills to zero in such fields as greenhouse gases, toxics, pandemics, and corruption.[4] To take just one example, and one in which our organizations have been involved, the Zero Discharge of Hazardous Chemicals initiative brings together sportswear brands, designers, and retailers to squeeze toxins out of supply chains, particularly in China. Part of the challenge here will be to help the Chinese take foreign advice to clean up their act, not easy even at a time when cities like Beijing and Shanghai are now routinely wreathed in killer smog. This is a stretch political challenge, not just a technical one. The hugely ambitious target elimination date: 2020.

This kind of ambition and stretch is now required of all of us. Indeed it is crucially important to learn from the late Steve Jobs's playbook, embracing "insanely ambitious" goals when it comes to fighting for a better future. Breakthrough leaders understand that even the best-intentioned incrementalism isn't going to crack it. Genuine, sustained system change is needed—and the recipes aren't always easily available from a change cookbook. Much of this we will have to make up as we go.

Work with Partners

Just as it is important to be ambitious and not to rely on others to drive transformative change, so it is equally important to encourage cooperation between those dissatisfied with the status quo, whatever their sector. New types of alliances and partnerships are key when it comes to putting in place the kinds of solutions and models that can be scaled, ideally globally.

Hannah Jones, vice president of sustainable business and innovation at Nike, is one breakthrough leader who has been looking for novel ways to partner with other organizations. Nike has linked up with NASA, for example, to explore novel materials. "Unconventional partnerships have always been a part of the way we innovate," she explains.

> LAUNCH is an association between NASA, USAID, and the U.S. State Department. The LAUNCH 2020 challenge aims to identify innovations in sustainable materials and methods of manufacturing. We purposefully brought the entire materials "system" into the room — about 150 scientists, NGOs, brands, academics, chemistry companies, manufacturers — to challenge siloed thinking and explore a true systemwide approach. Increasingly, leaders are recognizing that the scale of the changes required cannot be achieved by any individual entity. We have to find ways to redefine what is "precompetitive," where we can work together to advance innovative solutions in areas where we share risk and opportunity.

Muhammad Yunus, Nobel Prize winner, founder of the Grameen Bank, and a member of The B Team, agrees. He explains that without partnerships, much of the efforts of Grameen would have been ineffective, if not impossible. He notes that "my first venture was the Grameen Bank, which was not intended to make me rich or pay any dividend to me. I did not even wish to own a part or whole of it. Instead I set out to make the borrowers the owners of the bank. Even so, I was able to turn it into a big company, a sustainable company, focusing on something that was not done before. From there I moved into solar energy, getting renewable power into one and a half million homes. Then we created joint venture companies."

The range of initiatives expands continuously. "There are so many joint ventures now," Yunus notes. "Through one, with BASF, we are bringing mosquito nets to those heavily impacted by malaria, through another (with Uniqlo) we are bringing sanitary napkins to women in the villages. The best known of them is bringing nutrition to malnourished children of Bangladesh. This is a joint venture with Danone, the French food company. It focuses on developing and distributing nutritious yogurt products to poor children in Bangladesh." Danone's CEO, Franck Riboud, has reported that the project taught his company a great deal about everything from how to enter new markets and ways to design novel forms of packaging. The effort demonstrates that, when properly managed, social change and good business are in no way mutually exclusive.

Clearly, Grameen isn't the only organization that has embraced partnerships in an effort to build a more sustainable future. What is interesting, though, is the way that breakthrough leaders increasingly encourage their teams to learn from examples like this. Like the late C. K. Prahalad, who pioneered the concept of "bottom of the pyramid" markets, Yunus has been in great demand from corporate top teams wanting to know how they can play into this emerging opportunity space. In the process, the best of these people will stretch top-team assumptions and comfort zones to the limit.

Be Bold — and Simple

Being ambitious and working with partners does not call for complex, unwieldy solutions. Instead, The B Team encourages breakthrough leaders to be bold while working to catalyze simple, practical solutions that companies can share and replicate and, where it makes sense to do so, governments can help to incentivize.

Leaders in all sectors must identify and critically evaluate existing approaches, collaborators, and allies, with an eye both to simplification and effectiveness. Complex solutions are sometimes essential, but when ill-judged or poorly executed, they can hamstring even the most sophisticated organizations. The B Team encourages leaders to perform new comparative analyses of strategic options; to create, refine, and commit to selected strategies and solutions; and to agree to the necessary terms of reference, objectives, deliverables, and success metrics.

Redefine Success

Creative solutions that energize organizations and encourage them to work together require leaders and their organizations to rethink what it means to be successful over time. There are no guarantees of success in business, and certainly not when it comes to tackling the Breakthrough Challenge. The right aspirations in the wrong organization or at the wrong time can be a recipe for disaster. In contrast, the right aspirations at the right time and in the right sort of organization can provide a ticket to ride into a future that competitors simply can't get to or, in some cases, even see.

We must look beyond a healthy financial bottom line to an organization — or industry sector — that is healthy from top to bottom and contributes to wider health in the communities and environments in which it operates. (See Chapter Five.) This means embracing a holistic sense of well-being that looks not only at numbers and dollars but provides for employee welfare, protects safety and health, and promotes citizen engagement and human rights.

"We need to move beyond the current obsession with quarterly earnings and short-term growth—an obsession that too often comes at the expense of the long-term good of our individuals and communities," says Arianna Huffington, president and editor-in-chief of the Huffington Post Media Group and a member of The B Team. "We must redefine success to include well-being, wisdom, and service." In the process, well-being as a concept must be stretched beyond individuals, companies, communities, cities, and even countries to ecosystems and the global biosphere.

Catalyze Movements

The B Team understands that buy-in to Plan B can happen only when the concept begins to gain wider appeal. It is thus important for breakthrough leaders to look not only at themselves and their own organizations but also toward a larger world, one in which similar movements aggregate into a movement of movements. These leaders must work together to push everyone past a tipping point that tilts the future toward the Plan B vision.

Essentially, Plan B is about accelerating and guiding a global movement, not creating yet another institution. The B Team isn't trying to impose rules or guidelines. The ultimate aim is to get as many business leaders as possible—eventually millions of them—committed to radically better ways of doing business. Part of that commitment means that the leaders involved will also look critically at their own companies and business practices, leading by example and committing to accelerating a wider movement of business leaders around the world through their actions, not just their words.

Virgin Unite CEO Jean Oelwang has been involved from the very beginning of The B Team initiative. She explains that creating a movement in which breakthrough leaders join forces is a key tenet. "The idea emerged to bring together a group of business leaders whose collective global voice could help amplify the wonderful spectrum of hybrid businesses that are driven by purpose—and also help to inspire existing business leaders to truly transform their companies to make them engines for positive change in the world," she says. "We wanted The B Team to be a powerful force to help turn business upside down—and truly put people and planet at the core of the future of business. The collective voice and resources of this group will hopefully help give other leaders 'air cover' and help inspire millions of business leaders around the world to create a movement toward this new approach to business."

In the process, Plan B also calls for the development of a powerful new collective voice to fight for a better future—a voice for those who are prepared to move in good time and good order from the old ways to the new.

Provide a Voice for the Future

By acting now, being ambitious, working with partners, being bold, and redefining what success means, we can work together toward a world that embraces the Plan B agenda. This is the future that growing numbers of us want to create—indeed the future we must create. The B Team leaders are working to spread that message.

"My hope is that The B Team will help us create longer-term frameworks for capitalism, markets, and business," says Unilever CEO Paul Polman. "This agenda is a very tall order—and I would not pretend to have all the answers. But our strength as

The B Team will result from our combined voices, our credibility, and our reach."

This voice for the future is by no means limited to members of The B Team, however. It needs to become so powerful that it breaks the sustainability agenda out of its professional ghetto and makes it an irresistible global aspiration.

Engage People Around the World

It is imperative that Plan B not only serves but also includes young people around the world. We must project a mood of both realism and optimism, rather than succumbing to self-fulfilling pessimism. Young people often see the challenges—and the opportunities—more clearly than their elders, and many are already leading change efforts around the world. Their growing numbers, networked in new ways, increasingly have the capacity to effect systemic change. But their prospects will be immeasurably improved if those already in positions of influence and power find new ways to work with them.

Unilever CEO Paul Polman stresses that "we have to develop better means of leveraging social networks and youth. In Liberia, for example, 56 percent of the population are below fifteen years old—very hard to imagine. In the emerging markets, 50 percent of people are below twenty-five years old. They've realized they can utilize their skills and combine their efforts to create change. We see that with Arab Spring and Occupy Wall Street."

It is increasingly important to engage wider society when building toward a new future. Doing so will require breakthrough leaders to buy in to and help evolve the Plan B movement, and similar movements, to inspire tomorrow's leaders—those in emerging economies, like the BRICS and MINT nations,[5] or of established global powers—and guide them toward answers to the questions posed by the ever-expanding people-planet-profit agenda.

o Linking Aspirations to Incentives

These ten aspirations are no small order. Reaching these new horizons ultimately will require most business leaders to demonstrate that they can play a central role in developing and deploying solutions for a better, more sustainable future. They must earn — or in some cases re-earn — the trust, the social capital, needed to do so. They will need to secure their license to operate, to focus on the most essential challenges, and — above all — to innovate and to lead.

This historic process requires a root-and-branch review not just of corporate citizenship, corporate social responsibility, and new forms of shared value but also of business mind-sets and models and of emerging forms of both capital and capitalism. Daunting, certainly, but this is exactly the sort of challenge that true breakthrough leaders and innovators find most exciting, indeed irresistible.

The aspirations embedded in Plan B are inextricably linked to ambition and incentives, and The B Team aims to ensure that the right incentives are in place globally to promote, inspire, and reward business models that integrate people, planet, and profit into their DNA. For many people, being part of a new movement — for some just being in the game — is motivation enough. For others, it is the sheer size of the market opportunity that appeals.

Undeniably, money is a major incentive for many leaders. Indeed, for many organizations — and for their investors — it is the primary incentive (hence their continual focus on the financial bottom line). "Sitting on the Parliamentary Committee," recalls Justin Welby, the archbishop of Canterbury, "I really didn't think people would mind the difference between being paid £1 million and being paid £2 million, because they are such colossal sums of money. But bankers, quite openly, giving evidence in public, completely unaware of how it would be seen, said that £10 million to £12 million was not a lot of money. A year! For the first time, I thought 'I think I believe in genuine human greed.'"

Clearly, the sorts of incentives that attract and motivate different people, at different stages in their lives, at different moments in history, and up and down the Maslow Hierarchy of Needs can vary radically. The truth is, though, that many incentives in the current system conspire to maintain the old, dysfunctional order. Tomorrow's leaders must become much more adept at orchestrating the use of a wider spectrum of incentives and disincentives—carrots and sticks—to start, drive, and steer the economic, social, and political transformations the world now so urgently requires.

o Moving Aspirations Beyond Corporate Citizenship

When it comes to tackling issues of sustainability and well-being, many business organizations now talk about the importance of being good corporate citizens and about how necessary it is to be socially responsible and accountable. Corporate citizenship is generally considered as an agenda that encourages businesses to give back to the community, both locally and globally. Often, corporate responsibility is still tightly linked to philanthropy, particularly in the United States and many parts of Asia. Initiatives are funded by a sort of social tithe, a voluntary form of corporate taxation. Indeed, you can see corporate citizenship, corporate social responsibility, and responsible or conscious capitalism as forms of social lubrication to ensure that business maintains its license to operate, focus, and innovate.

All well worth having—and these social outcomes have been hard fought for. Nevertheless, these days corporate citizenship and corporate social responsibility are increasingly disparaged by breakthrough leaders as too little, too late. Although small steps are crucial in any journey, and the record confirms that these initiatives can help prepare the ground for breakthrough, the truth is that too often they can be like applying a Band-Aid or taking a painkiller when radical surgery is needed. Another weakness of these agendas, as we noted earlier, is that they often enjoy little traction in the world's boardrooms and C-suites. Their budgets are small, their link to corporate strategy is weak, and their ability to shape the underlying business model is often virtually nonexistent.

That is why we need to think about breakthrough innovation, breakthrough entrepreneurship, and breakthrough capitalism. As we move to embrace — and perform against — tomorrow's bottom line, leaders must recognize that CSR and other boardroom buzzwords are in danger of becoming obsolete ambitions — or, more likely, will become something more basic, the entry ticket to a higher-stakes game.

We need radically new thinking about capitalism, as well as about the various forms of capital. Specifically, breakthrough leaders aim to get a better grip on what the human, intellectual, social, and natural forms of capital mean for the future of their organizations. They must consider the cost of these different forms of capital and the effects that using (and misusing) currently nonfinancial forms of capital have on people and the planet. Doing so will require a profound change in the way we think, prioritize, operate, and lead. It also will require changes in the rules and dynamics of the economic system itself. This, in turn, means creating new corporate structures, and we'll look at that challenge next, in Chapter Two.

2

Create New Corporate
Structures

It will be impossible to fully address the Breakthrough Challenge without tackling the issue of how business is structured and owned. Current corporate structures and ownership patterns routinely fail to provide the kind of flexibility that organizations need in order to be innovative, resilient, and sustainable over the long term.

Restructurings, reorganizations, mergers, and acquisitions may temporarily inject new life and energy into particular corporations and sectors, briefly permitting a new focus on the long term, but the short-term mind-set of current structures—and of the financial markets to which so many of them are in thrall—means that they can still be dangerously myopic. According to Michael Townsend, founder and CEO of Earthshine Solutions, "all this takes place within a conventional paradigm, and is really just rearranging the deckchairs."[1]

Like it or not, today's economy is headed toward a tipping point no less profound than that triggered by the advent of

Communism. The question, once again, is whether capitalism will choose to evolve, whether it will be forced to make the necessary changes, or whether it will be abandoned along the wayside. Breakthrough leaders know that the challenge we face is systemic, way beyond the reach of even the most ambitious stakeholder reporting and engagement. They conclude that a new business paradigm is now essential if we are to break free of short-term thinking about making profits and to embrace long-term thinking, strategies, and business models that better address the Breakthrough Challenge.

Moving far beyond efficiency and responsibility measures, The B Team concludes that the time has come to accelerate the evolution and adoption of new corporate structures and ownership patterns. This will be one of our toughest challenges, yet it will be crucial if we are to create the sort of systemic solutions now needed to address the world's accelerating environmental, social, and governance problems.

Those who stick with the old corporate structures risk finding themselves tethered to an increasingly dysfunctional status quo — an option that is likely to lead nowhere good as the economy itself goes through fundamental structural changes. Most forms of corporate structure today dictate the kind of short-termism that places people and the planet far behind profitability. In some jurisdictions, strikingly, fiduciary duty is interpreted as insisting that financial considerations dominate all others. As a result, most current forms of ownership focus solely on the interests of shareholders, with for-profit business organizations required to boost their return on financial investment — and ditto their quarterly earnings — in order to meet intensifying analyst expectations and wider market demands. Such market realities make it difficult, if not impossible, to break out from today's mind-sets and models to create value in more sustainable ways.

Concepts like limited liability, shareholder value, and fiduciary duty have generally served us well in the past, but the time has come to take a close, critical look at some of the core principles of business and capitalism in order to begin to evolve toward more equitable and sustainable ways of creating and distributing value. In the process, we need to look at new forms of corporate structure and ownership that can stimulate entrepreneurship and innovation while at the same time considering the needs of all key stakeholders. As we move into what many scientists now call the Anthropocene, in which our species instigates geological-scale impacts, we must also consider the needs of our atmosphere and biosphere.

Happily, some promising options are emerging, which—if embraced in good time and good order—can lead us toward forms of value creation far better suited to the new century's very different political, social, environmental, and economic realities.

o Existing — and Breakthrough — Corporate Forms

The private sector, financial markets, and governments all must become much better at nurturing different styles of businesses. Social businesses, B Corporations (or B Corps), cooperatives, family-owned businesses, state-owned enterprises, and other formats already play important roles in today's global economy. We need a period of experimentation in business akin to the Cambrian explosion, which saw life evolve new structures, physiologies, and capabilities.

That said, most breakthrough leaders would readily admit that no corporate structure is without fault. Every option in the broadening spectrum of ownership structures has its own weaknesses, some of which may not become clear until it is in widespread use. For example, although family-owned businesses can think longer term, often because they are free of at least some of the constraints of the public capital markets, they often are less experienced with the disciplining effects of transparency mechanisms. Similarly, state-owned enterprises can sometimes rise above the vagaries of the market, but they can also become arrogant, inward looking, nationalistic, and elitist.

So let's examine some of the forms, traditional and transformational, that help structure business activities today, and consider how they may play a role in shaping and implementing the Plan B agenda.

LLCs

One pervasive—and persistent—corporate structure is the limited liability company (LLC). LLCs provide legal benefits and tax advantages that make them appealing to companies across industries and geographies. No surprise, then, that this has consistently been one of the most widely used corporate formats. However, somewhat to the surprise of its most energetic champions, the LLC concept has faced intensifying challenges in recent years. For example, costs that ought to have flowed to the owners and operators of a given company have been cascaded to the wider world as economic, social, and environmental externalities.

With increasing pressure on resources and an emerging paradigm that requires a very different set of relationships with people and the planet, LLCs will eventually have to internalize these externalities. Happily, the upside is that this is likely to spur much innovation, even if the downside is that it will prove the undoing of many incumbent organizations and even industries.

That said, no one sees the LLC story ending. More likely this long-surviving corporate form will be adapted for new needs, rather than being abandoned along the wayside. One key reason for that forecast is that it is not yet totally clear what forms or structures might replace the LLC.

Family-Owned Businesses

Although they tend to operate to one side of the media spotlight, family-owned businesses include some of the world's longest-running organizations as well as some of the world's largest companies, among them Wal-Mart, Koch Industries, Cargill, Samsung, and the Tata Group. As one of the most popular forms of corporate structure, family-owned businesses are often marked by agility, ingenuity, and trust (although none of these are givens).

On the other side of that coin can be nepotism, family feuding, and weak succession planning. Still, family-owned businesses can provide a level of flexibility that LLCs and other traditional corporate forms often struggle to achieve. They may well offer growing numbers of breakthrough leaders — and other change agents — the latitude to think longer term as they plan and invest to help build a more sustainable future.

Employee-Owned Businesses

Employee-owned businesses — a significant, if often invisible, feature in the economic landscape — represent yet another approach, one in which the involvement of employees can bring stability and longer-term thinking, at least when implemented well. In employee-owned businesses, by definition, some or all of the employees are co-owners, and as a result they can exercise a fair amount of influence in deciding how profits are allocated and invested. Often a much greater share of profits and dividends may flow to these employees rather than to outside shareholders. As a result, it is often the case that employee-owned businesses generate higher employee loyalty, improved productivity, and increased profits.

Interestingly, too, a new index shows that employee share ownership can deliver substantially better returns for investors than their publicly listed peers. The UK Employee Share Owner-ship Index tracks the share price performance of FTSE All-Share companies where employees own more than 3 percent of the total equity.[2] In 2013, the shares in sixty-nine companies that met this employee ownership condition delivered returns of 53.3 percent, on average, compared with an average of 20.9 percent from the remaining 623 companies in the All-Share index. Senior executives in the sector conclude that among the factors in play are increased employee motivation, lower staff attrition rates, and easier recruitment.

On the flip side, however, employee-owned businesses can suffer from being overly leveraged (though that is by no means unique to them) and from experiencing more than the usual volume of conflicts of interest. Still, in areas of the world with the right sort of business environment, employee-owned concerns may well encourage the sort of longer-term thinking and greater cooperation the future is likely to depend on.

Cooperatives

Like employee-owned businesses, cooperatives tend to be rela-tively small and quite nimble, yet they also potentially provide the flexibility required for long-term thinking. They are owned by and operated for the benefit of those using their services. Common in agriculture, health care, and retail, cooperatives distribute their profits and earnings among members rather than to outside shareholders.

Stand back and it is clear that the scale of the cooperative sec-tor is enormous. Already a decade ago, in 2004, the Global 300 report indicated that the top cooperatives in the world had total revenues of around $1 trillion.[3] Today, cooperatives boast more than a billion members worldwide and more than one hundred million employees.[4]

Because they exist for the benefit of members rather than to generate profits for investors, cooperatives tend to take a longer-term view, focusing not just on the financial bottom line but also on the long-term sustainability of the business and the well-being of employees. Potentially, this is right in line with the people-planet-profit agenda.

Social Businesses and B Corps

Like cooperatives, which have been around for quite some time, a variety of new forms of social business are now booming. As noted in the Introduction, a social business is typically one where a non-dividend company is created to solve a social problem. Like any business, it generates its own revenues to cover costs. Profits, generally, are reinvested rather than distributed to investors.

Muhammad Yunus, founder of the Grameen Bank and a member of The B Team, insists that all revenues should be put back into the social business, although some others in the field believe that it is perfectly acceptable for some financial dividends to be distributed to investors. Indeed, not just acceptable but necessary, given that the prospect of at least some financial payback can help attract types of funding that would otherwise be inaccessible.

Either way, social businesses represent an increasingly exciting option for breakthrough-oriented leaders wanting to push through to the next generation of value creation.

Another new corporate format is the B Corporation, mentioned earlier and discussed briefly in the Introduction. The B Corp approach is being adopted by a growing number of for-profit, social-mission businesses, largely because it provides a robust, integrated approach to aligning businesses with social and environmental interests. By way of context, both of the companies one of us (John Elkington) is involved in running, SustainAbility and Volans, are now certified B Corps. (Volans was the second to be so certified in the United Kingdom, SustainAbility the third.)

B Corps adopt corporate missions that encompass social and environmental impact, governance structures that support that mission and measurement, and forms of transparency in relation to their social and environmental impact that are based on a comparable yardstick. No specific ownership format is prescribed, but the adoption of new B Corp–friendly legislation in many U.S. states, including Delaware, undermines the old arguments there that fiduciary duty means that corporations can only, by law, focus on the financial bottom line — and, longer term, potentially throws such arguments out the window.

By design, B Corps voluntarily meet high standards of accountability, corporate purpose, and transparency. They "have a corporate purpose to create a material positive impact on society and the environment; . . . are required to consider the impact of their decisions not only on shareholders but also on workers, community, and the environment; and . . . are required to make available to the public an annual benefit report that assesses their overall social and environmental performance against a third party standard."[5]

The B Corp formula is promoted by B Lab, a nonprofit that serves a growing global movement of entrepreneurs using the power of business to solve social and environmental problems. According to B Lab, "B Corp certification is to sustainable business what Fair Trade certification is to coffee or USDA Organic certification is to milk. These organizations are certified by the nonprofit B Lab to meet rigorous standards of social and environmental performance, accountability, and transparency. Today, there is a growing community of more than 850 certified B Corps from 28 countries and 60 industries working together toward one unifying goal: to redefine success in business."[6]

B Lab board member Debra Dunn, associate professor at the Stanford d.school (that's *d* as in "design"), has the advantage of having worked both in a very large corporation (Hewlett-Packard) and, increasingly, in the B Corp space. Her experience in the profit and nonprofit worlds helps shed light on some key issues. "First," she explains, "we have no hope of tackling the major social and environmental issues that we face without the full participation of the business sector. And, second, building social responsibility into the DNA of a company is simply inadequate. We need a new construct for business because at the end of the day, shareholder primacy can completely trump social responsibility."

Dunn—alongside the members of The B Team—concludes that B Corps offer a robust, integrated approach to aligning businesses with social and environmental interests. Again, B Corporation certification takes things up a notch by requiring organizations to craft—and adhere to—a tailored corporate mission that encompasses social and environmental impact, a supportive governance structure, and real overall transparency.

Dave Chen, also a B Lab board member and cofounder and principal at Equilibrium Capital, latched on to the B Corp concept in 2008 when Equilibrium Capital Group was working to define a corporate structure for the firm that would allow it to fulfill and retain its mission for the long haul. The B Corp model appealed to him because it provided an opportunity to change the organization's corporate law framework and, he says, "the sometime stifling definition of 'fiduciary duty.'"

Chen explains that the B Corp format and certification process helped Equilibrium focus its mission. "I liken [the certification process] to ISO standards, a process of improvement and benchmarking," he says. "The adoption of the law in a growing number of states across the United States changes the scope of fiduciary duty, giving the B Corp the protection of the law for making choices that consider factors beyond shareholder value. In some ways, I would argue that becoming a legal benefit corporation actually heightens the bar for fiduciary duty." This is encouraging, particularly because raising the bar on fiduciary duty is a key goal of the Plan B approach.

B Corps provide leaders with a new option for crafting a corporate structure that will help them tackle the Breakthrough Challenge—not that adopting this new form will be easy. Dunn stresses that one of the most demanding tasks for B Corps is "striking the right balance between keeping the bar high and scaling as quickly as possible. We are very open and transparent in our approach and want as many organizations as possible to use the B ratings system (also known as 'GIIRS') to assess and improve their organizations even if they don't choose to become certified B Corps," she says. "We also want to build the community of certified B Corps as quickly as possible, because scale increases our effectiveness in influencing policy, consumer behavior, and even public companies. We need to make B [Corp status] accessible while maintaining its integrity."

In order for B Corps to gain even more traction, the structure has to be applicable to mainstream, large-scale businesses. "The entire B Corp model is absolutely workable for big companies, though getting a current public company to adopt it is almost implausible because the shareholders would have to agree to give up their primacy," Dunn notes. Implausible, but not impossible; it is worth noting that Unilever subsidiary Ben & Jerry's has been certified as a B Corp. Of course, Ben & Jerry's isn't a plain vanilla company, nor is Patagonia, which has also taken the B Corp route. However, there is growing evidence that the B Corp approach can shape the wider debate about how businesses are best configured for the future.

○ Rethinking Existing Business Structures

Existing businesses, particularly those with entrenched legacy issues, may find it impossible to adopt wholly new corporate structures. They will insist that doing so is possible only for new organizations. This doesn't mean, however, that big businesses can't adopt at least some new-structure thinking that can help them better serve the people-planet-profit agenda. For example, organizations can acquire more sustainable businesses, as Unilever acquired Ben & Jerry's and Coca-Cola acquired Innocent, a quirky, people-planet-profit-oriented smoothie maker that embraces what it calls a "chain of good," as in the product tastes good, does you good, and helps do good for others.[7]

Other companies insist that they can tackle environmental, social, and governance challenges within current ownership structures. One example is Nestlé, which adopted what it called its Creating Shared Value approach at the urging of then-CEO Peter Brabeck-Letmathe, later the company's chairman. He is one of a growing number of business leaders who have awakened to the strategic importance of the wider societal agenda, moving first to organizational changes and then on to wider advocacy.

Shared value recognizes the importance of "the intersection between society and corporate performance." As noted by Michael E. Porter and Mark R. Kramer in their article "Creating Shared Value," it requires of leaders "a far deeper appreciation of societal needs, a greater understanding of the true bases of company productivity, and the ability to collaborate across profit/nonprofit boundaries."[8]

Brabeck-Letmathe admits that there were some challenges when it came to, for example, integrating multiple forms of value into the balance sheet. In order to tackle those challenges, he realized that he needed to engage busy leaders in both the private and public sectors by tying shared value into broader initiatives. "In leading companies, we have increasingly seen the conscious integration of societal values into business strategies," he says. In addition, there is "a greater acceptance of the need to integrate the private sector into the once-exclusive development efforts of governments and NGOs. These trends have helped the world to move more efficiently forward in implementing the UN Millennium Development Goals."

Here a different form of ownership is at play, with such companies increasingly feeling a sense of ownership of society's wider ethical, social, and environmental objectives. The shared value approach is one among a number of ways in which breakthrough leaders can help push their organizations forward, though backing from Porter and Kramer has helped turn Nestlé's approach into an increasingly powerful international movement.

By helping leaders reframe citizenship issues as business challenges, shared value is a potential game changer. Critics of the approach, however, note that it generally focuses on win-win outcomes. These are devoutly to be desired, of course, but are a lot less likely if you expand the analysis to look at wider system dysfunctions. You could have wonderful socioeconomic outcomes, for example, as the ecosystems that underpinned the relevant growth crumbled under the weight of exploitation.

Take the increasingly heated issue of climate change. There are an immense number of win-win energy-efficiency and carbon-offset solutions going begging in such areas, suggesting huge shared value opportunities, but climate change is also a symptom of wider failures in economics, valuation, accounting, and governance. Addressing such failures will mean that at least some people face major losses, with so-called stranded assets likely to be a growing headache in the coming decades in areas like the fossil fuels sector. Rather than win-win outcomes, here we are talking about win-lose and lose-lose outcomes that will generate intense political debate and counterlobbying from those with most at stake. These won't be losses just for coal barons: many ordinary people have their pensions invested, at least to some degree, in coal and other fossil fuel stocks and shares.

In such cases, there will be no substitute for strong, coherent, and sustained political leadership from political leaders, governments, and policymakers. Breakthrough business leaders can help drive the process along. They can, for example, ensure that their lobbying activities, both direct and indirect, align with their wider goals. Other options include supporting future changes to the structures and requirements of public markets. For example, Nestlé has long refused to issue quarterly earnings guidance. Similarly, Unilever's Paul Polman announced in 2009 when he became CEO that he would abolish guidance as well as quarterly reporting. This does not mean that such companies are without fault—no organization is—but the key point here is that they are using at least some of their influence to help catalyze wider system change.

○ Achieving Buy-In for Tomorrow's Corporate Forms

It can be hugely difficult—where it is possible at all—to change corporate structures once they are established and in wide use. Inching toward new formats is certainly an option, though whole-scale restructuring can also be forced on companies that have allowed themselves to become significantly out of step with wider markets.

Some publicly listed organizations may choose to go private, as Richard Branson did with Virgin and as the founders of The Body Shop International, Anita and Gordon Roddick, considered doing when they found that being publicly listed got in the way of their wider ethical, social, and environmental goals. Others may decide to explore new value creation strategies and ownership formats by moving into corporate venturing, an option that may help avoid unsettling too many investors.

Breakthrough leaders understand that the key is to engage and motivate their top teams—and the wider world of business leadership, which we dub the "global C-suite." Made up of the world's top one thousand corporations, the global C-suite is critically important, "because of the tremendous increase of concentration of economic activity that has occurred in this group over the past thirty years. They are a powerful force for creating positive outcomes and negative externalities," as Harvard Business School professor Bob Eccles explains.

Whatever for-profit format is used, Brabeck-Letmathe of Nestlé notes that "senior leaders must focus on long-term sustainable business goals and practices, since long-term business thinking leads directly to creating shareholder value, together with real social progress. Interest is growing in this approach, but many barriers remain to long-term thinking—not the least of which is the reporting of quarterly earnings and a focus on short-term profit maximization."

Underscoring a theme to which we will return in Chapter Ten, Brabeck-Letmathe notes that "corporate executives need to be incentivized to think longer term." This involves changing executive compensation plans, rewarding long-term shareholder value creation, and advancing public policy changes that help focus companies on the long term. It also takes breakthrough leaders who have the strength to resist an exclusive focus on the short term, working to create acceptable short-term profits while executing long-term plans for sustainable shareholder value.

These efforts clearly start with, but go well beyond, the CEO. New corporate structures also require buy-in from sales, marketing, communications, and R&D. In short, the people-planet-profit agenda has to be championed at all levels of the organization across functional, business, and geographic groups.

○ Achieving Critical Mass

Asking organizations to adopt wholly new corporate structures is challenging in the best of times. Breakthrough leaders report that convincing their business peers that a shift is needed to new corporate formats takes unusual dedication and determination from top teams, but it also requires buy-in from those outside the business.

Leaders must encourage and support efforts on the part of business schools. (We'll talk more about redefining education in Chapter Eight.) They also can call for more favorable government incentives for particular ownership formats, such as support for social enterprise, either through tax breaks or by favoring social enterprises in public purchasing decisions and specifications. The biggest changes will come in the form of new business chartering rules, new tax and regulatory regimes, and new public sector purchasing specifications and rules. In Chapter Six, we'll take a closer look at what governments can do to help on this front.

Beyond business schools and government, breakthrough leaders look to other organizations to support the push toward new corporate forms. One way forward is to encourage other platforms they are involved in (for example, trade associations, the World Economic Forum, the World Business Council for Sustainable Development, or the Clinton Global Initiative) to dig into this area and to work on breakthrough solutions.

Ultimately, however, implementing new corporate structures is only one step toward advancing the goals of Plan B. Success with the Breakthrough Challenge also will require leaders and their organizations to be much more accountable, measuring the external costs of doing business, considering wider system dynamics, and evolving timely and effective change strategies. We'll tackle those issues next, in Chapter Three.

3

Apply True Accounting
Principles

Accountants may seem to be unlikely agents of market transformation, but they—and their discipline—are central to Plan B. Some leaders, including some very successful ones, insist that they operate from their gut, using their instincts and intuition, but even they must often turn to the numbers to see how they are doing—and most people in business, the financial markets, and the public sector depend on the latest numbers provided by their organizational dashboards as they navigate, steer, brake, and accelerate their way through the obstacle courses set by modern markets.

By their very nature and training, most accountants are conservative. They are encouraged—indeed generally required—to look backward rather than forward. Creative accounting is rarely encouraged because of the mayhem it can cause in business and our economies. Accountants aim to boil down relevant information into financial numbers, with anything that cannot be quantified in this way likely to be shunted into the margins or small print, at best. They operate a system that they did not design, but for which they see themselves not just as professional operators but also as part of a long line of trusted custodians.

All of which is fine and as it should be, except that the field of accounting is going through a fundamental — if protracted — paradigm shift. This is partly signaled by the growing use of terms like ethical, social, or environmental accounting; full cost accounting; and double, triple, and even quadruple bottom lines. It is also accompanied by the dawning realization that our economies will have to account for progress (or the lack of it) at every level of value creation and impact. In today's increasingly globalized value chains, with investment, production, and consumption activities dispersed around the globe, the task is becoming very much more complicated.

Business leaders — and, as a result, accountants — increasingly must measure the creation, use, or erosion of an ever-broader spectrum of different forms of capital. Traditionally, of course, these have been the physical and financial forms, but in recent years we have seen an intensifying push for a more sophisticated consideration of human and intellectual capital, and also now for both social and natural capital. Nor is that the end of it: another form is institutional capital, which provides the context within which business operates. Embracing, integrating, and accounting for all the relevant forms of capital represents the core challenge for the future of capitalism in general, and for business leaders and accountants in particular.

In what follows, we will briefly review the emergence of conventional, single-bottom-line accounting, exploring one dimension of corporate performance. Then we consider some trends that have been pushing us toward multiple-bottom-line forms of accounting, management, and reporting. Finally, we argue the need for a "multidimensional" model of accounting, which will embrace new horizontal and vertical aspects and track them through time, the fourth dimension. As we shall see, it is this fourth dimension — time — that brings a broadening range of system-level issues into sharper focus.

○ Accounting for Profit and Loss

The evolution of financial accounting has been one of humankind's greatest achievements. The story is wonderfully told in Jane Gleeson-White's book *Double Entry: How the Merchants of Venice Created Modern Finance.*[1] The discipline's roots can be tracked way back to the clay tablets used in ancient Babylonian times to record trading and business deals, among other things. Much later, in the 1490s, the Franciscan friar Luca Pacioli popularized the basic accounting method, double-entry bookkeeping, used by Venetian traders. This method balanced assets and liabilities to produce an assessment of the performance of a given business.

These days, a business is likely to be required to produce a balance sheet, which reports on an organization's assets, liabilities, and ownership equity at a given point in time. It also may need to prepare an income statement — also sometimes called a profit and loss account, a statement of earnings or financial performance, or an operating statement — which indicates how the revenues (received from sales of products or services, before expenses are taken into account, often referred to as the "top line") are transformed into income, at which point all revenues and expenses have been accounted for. This describes the "net profit" or "bottom line."

Confusing though all this may be to some, certain clear principles underlie what accountants do. Type "accounting principles" into a search engine like Google, and you are likely to come up with a wealth of links to websites, papers, and articles using a bewildering array of acronyms. Among them will be GAAP (generally accepted accounting principles), which guide much business-level accounting today.[2] This book is not the place to run through all the principles involved in GAAP-style accounting, but several are worth highlighting to illustrate both the strengths and weaknesses of traditional forms of accounting:

1. **The economic entity assumption.** Under this heading, the accountant aims to keep all the business transactions of a business's owner separate from the owner's personal transactions. This is essential to avoid the corruption of a company by the potentially distorting personal interests of owners.

2. **The monetary unit assumption.** This dictates that the transactions undertaken by a business can only be expressed in the currency of the nation-state in which the business is based. This assumption makes no provision for the recording of things like units of carbon emitted into the atmosphere, for example, or of indicators of the safety, health, and well-being of employees.

3. **The time period assumption.** Time periods are generally expressed in terms of quarters or financial years. The problem here is that many ethical, social, and environmental issues develop over many years or decades.

4. **The full disclosure principle.** This is likely to be the foundation stone for much multidimensional accounting and reporting. If certain information is potentially important to investors or lenders — typically facts likely to cause financial consequences in the timescales relevant to the business and its investors and lenders — it should be disclosed in the accountant's statement or in the footnotes. If a company faces a lawsuit in response to alleged ethical, social, or environmental failures, that would need to be referenced, but currently there is no requirement to include such issues in their own right.

5. **The principle of materiality.** Deciding whether an amount to be accounted for, either as an expense or as income, is insignificant or immaterial, in the sense that it will have little impact on the state or health of the business, requires professional judgment. Materiality is an accounting principle that has attracted a great deal of attention from people in the fields of corporate social responsibility and sustainability, on the basis that today's materiality assessments can miss a range of external (or externalized) factors that become more significant to the business — or to society or the environment — over time.

6. **The going concern principle.** This is particularly significant because it assumes that a business will exist long enough to carry out its objectives and contracted commitments — or, to put it another way, that it will not choose or be forced to liquidate in the foreseeable future. If the financial situation is such that the accountant believes there is a real risk to the continued survival of the business, then he or she is required to disclose this assessment. Imagine what would happen if this principle were to be stretched to consider factors that might undermine the company's business model or value proposition over time, including a range of externalities that might come home to roost, as they did for the asbestos and CFC industries.

Such principles distill the collective wisdom that accountants and the business community have developed over generations, but evidence suggests that there are intrinsic weaknesses in the way that some — or all — are defined. Indeed, Gleeson-White warns that something has gone horribly wrong in modern accounting: "From the notorious implosion in 2001 of the 1990s 'It Company,' the energy giant Enron, to the near collapse of the global financial markets in 2008, we have witnessed a wave of spectacular cases of profoundly misleading, inscrutable and flawed corporate accounting." One after another, she says, "the behemoths of finance and banking toppled—Lehman Brothers, HBOS, AIG, Anglo Irish Bank, the Icelandic banks Glitnir and Landsbank—all struck down by 'gigantic holes' that appeared, apparently out of nowhere, on the asset side of their balance sheets. And on their way down, these giants brought the international finance system to its knees."[3]

Gleeson-White notes that our entire economic system is now teetering on the edge of a new set of gigantic holes. Having considered our progress since the work of Luca Pacioli more than five hundred years ago, she concludes that flawed accounting and bookkeeping now have the potential to make or break not just companies or economies but our planet itself. Because accounting reduces everything to its monetary value, it has allowed us to value least that apparently free source of life itself, Earth. "Through its logic," she notes, "we have let the planet go to ruin—and through its logic we now have a chance to avert that ruin."[4]

The existing order systematically undervalues—or fails to value at all—key aspects of the people-planet-profit agenda. Most existing processes of economics, valuation, pricing, and accounting favor improving financial performance, growing financial returns, and increasing financial dividends over nonfinancial aspects and most intangibles. So before we turn to multidimensional accounting, let's take a quick look at a story that illustrates how even the most exciting breakthroughs in science, technology, and business models can generate the darkest clouds to match their silver linings.

o Probing the Dark Side of Accounting

No question, capitalism has brought us many benefits that would have been unimaginable to previous generations. Many of us would not be alive today without the miracles achieved by pioneers in science, technology, and business, including breakthrough inventions and innovations that have helped feed, house, and fuel the world's burgeoning human population. However, such achievements have often come at a cost—a cost that is rarely taken into account in the ledgers of the industries and companies that have led the charge.

Consider just one example, that of the ingenious Haber-Bosch process that appeared a century ago as a powerful way to synthesize ammonia. The process, which uses nitrogen from the atmosphere to create fertilizers, has helped feed billions of people. "Bread from air," was an eye-catching early slogan advertising the work of chemist Fritz Haber. Late in 2013, however, when several hundred scientists gathered in Ludwigshafen, Germany, they helped shine a light on the darker sides of one of the previous century's most extraordinary breakthroughs.[5]

Pretty much the same process was used to create explosives estimated to have killed as many as one hundred million people. It was also employed to make gas weapons used in World War I and the Zyklon B used to kill more than a million people in the World War II gas chambers, including members of Haber's own extended family. Worse, even the upsides of the story turn out to have downsides. For example, synthetic fertilizers have helped swell the global population, though that modern miracle has been achieved at the expense of increasingly elbowing the natural world aside—and polluting what remains with runoff fertilizers and insecticides. Great dead zones have emerged on the sea floor off the Mississippi Delta, to take just one example of the unforeseen effects of this form of industrial chemistry.

A simple indication of the pervasiveness of the technology's impact today is that it is estimated that half the nitrogen atoms in our bodies originally came from a Haber factory. In whose set of numbers does that inconvenient fact appear? What would

Fritz Haber have done had he had access to such numbers and projections when he was developing his process? Put aside the implications for his own family for the moment. If he had been able to see the other consequences and had nonetheless decided to push ahead, he—and the wider society—would at least have been better prepared for what came next.

A particularly dramatic example, no question, but The B Team concludes that leaders pursuing breakthrough trajectories, whatever their sector and their priority issues, whatever sort of business or organization they may be running, need to accept new forms of responsibility and accountability to people, to society, and to the planet, today and tomorrow.

Plan B requires that leaders focus not only on the organization, its brand, its values, and its legacy but also on employees and shareholders—indeed, on all key stakeholders. Unlike the Fritz Habers of the past, today's breakthrough leaders know that they must broaden their focus to take in their supply chains and value webs, and extend their time horizons far beyond the norm.

In this spirit, a small but growing number of leaders acknowledge that they will have to work out how to hold themselves accountable to the interests of future generations. Bill McKibben, the astonishingly influential writer–turned–investment activist who runs 350.org, refers to what he calls "the bottomest of bottom lines." He notes that "the question for a century has been, 'Does this lead to economic growth?' If yes, then we did it." Now, he says, the question has to be, "Does this lead to an increased chance of civilizational survival?" This is a question that today's accountants are ill-prepared to answer, but the increasing global interest in multidimensional management, accounting, and reporting represents an emerging context for their work that they—and we—would be ill-advised to ignore.

○ Accounting in Multiple Dimensions

Much of what currently passes for multidimensional accounting and reporting is poorly rooted in data; poorly integrated (if it is integrated at all) in the management, accounting, and reporting systems of companies; and often lacking the sort of information on (and connections to) the wider sustainability context that would make the resulting numbers meaningful and useful. Too often, management, accounting, and reporting systems operate in separate silos. The challenge is complicated when the focus widens to take into account the activities of the relevant companies' globalized value chains, right back to the suppliers of basic resources and right forward to the last user before a product ends up in the waste stream.

As a result, The B Team concludes that the principles underlying tomorrow's accounting and reporting will need to be vastly different in terms of the time periods over which value creation (or erosion) should be considered, and in terms of such principles as full disclosure, materiality, and going concern. It is time to account in multiple dimensions and, in the process, turn the powerful, unsettling lenses of "true accounting" onto everything that we do.

If we are to encourage organizations across countries and sectors to account for the true costs and impacts of their business activities, we must evolve new methods and tools that those organizations can use to set new priorities and push toward transformational targets. Currently, wider economic, social, and environmental impacts are still largely covered in anecdotal fashion. By contrast, business needs practical tools that it can use and integrate into its day-to-day operations. Finding ways to monetize, measure, and manage the full range of impacts that businesses produce throughout their organizations, supply chains, and value webs will be a crucial step toward true accounting.

63

Financial markets, so far, have shown little—and in some cases zero—interest in measuring these impacts because the evidence of the darker side of capitalism is absent, weak, or contested, often by those with most to lose from transformational change. Unless there are clear regulatory constraints or guidelines (or some likelihood that there will be over time), most analysts, financial organizations, and CFOs have little in the way of market incentives to factor in the costs of their economic, social, and environmental externalities.

Meanwhile, even the most committed C-suite executives rarely volunteer serious, contextualized information about the issues they are now beginning to track in their accounting and reporting. This is partly because they don't believe that analysts and shareholders are interested, but also partly because executives often don't yet know or understand what they should be measuring—or how to do so. So let's now look at some of the most important new accounting methods available for leaders aspiring to embrace the Breakthrough Challenge.

Reporting Environmental Footprints

Natural capital accounting tracks the total stocks and flows of natural resources, including the health of ecosystems and, ultimately, of the biosphere. As such, it is best done by governments—and there have been a growing number of studies and index initiatives designed to assess the nature, scale, health, and value of the natural capital of particular countries and even regions. This is work that still has many years to run before we can routinely and reliably monitor, account for, and report on the relevant trends. Eventually, such data will be factored into estimates of gross national product, alongside progress (or lack of it) in terms of the creation, use, and depreciation of other forms of capital.

This is the context within which businesses will increasingly be called on to report on their environmental footprints—and on the implications of their activities for the wider world of natural capital. To be fit for the future, accounting must embrace systemwide environmental, social, and governance effects resulting from the actions of individual economic actors that historically would have been able to ignore those effects. A few corporate reporters already are reaching in that direction, but the global infrastructure is not yet in place to make systemwide sense of what they are reporting—let alone provide feedback or instructions regarding which remedial actions the relevant companies should be taking.

One key player in the reporting space is Trucost, which compiles data and insight to help its clients identify their natural capital dependency across companies, products, supply chains, and investments. It also helps them manage risks linked to volatile commodity prices and increasing environmental costs. The key is not just to quantify natural capital dependency but also to put a price on it, helping clients understand environmental risk in business terms. Richard Mattison, CEO of Trucost, explains that "natural capital accounting can be used by companies to assess natural capital risk and opportunity embedded within their operations and supply chains." Natural capital accounting resonates with a small but growing number of companies, and is likely to do so over time with their investors and with governments.

Research has found that the natural capital impacts of the world's largest companies cost the global economy around $7.3 trillion per year, representing a systemic financial risk larger than that faced during the global financial crisis that began in 2008, which wiped $5.4 trillion off the value of Organization for Economic Cooperation and Development (OECD) pension funds in 2008.[6] You won't find that reported by the companies themselves; however, if we extended disclosure and materiality principles of GAAP across decades rather than years, the implications would be clear for all to see. Many businesses do not currently generate sufficient profit to cover their natural resource and pollution impacts, if these costs had to be paid for by the company. For example, the natural capital cost of cattle ranching in the southern United States is more than nineteen times the sector revenue for that region.[7]

In its first environmental profit and loss (EP&L) assessment, German sportswear company Puma calculated that the environmental impact for the areas it had identified as most significant (and, as a result, financially material), including the greenhouse gas emissions, water use, land use, air pollution, and waste generated through its operations and supply chain, ought to have had a price tag of at least €145 million in 2010. This represented around half of the company's profits that year. The first round of evaluation also revealed that Puma's wider supply chain was responsible for 94 percent (or €137 million) of the company's total environmental impact.

Strikingly, more than half (57 percent, or €83 million) of all environmental impacts were associated with the production of raw materials (including leather, cotton, and rubber), deep down in the company's supply chain. It also turned out that only 6 percent of the total identified impacts (valued at €8 million) derived from Puma's core operations, such as offices, warehouses, stores, and logistics, with greenhouse gases making up 90 percent of the impact of the company's offices, stores, and warehouses. Puma's owner, Kering, is now developing EP&L accounts for its other brands, including Gucci, Bottega Veneta, and Stella McCartney.

Integrated Accounting

Mainstream accountancy firms — and others — are experimenting with linked frameworks to bring together the various dimensions of value creation (or destruction) into an increasingly integrated approach. PwC, which helped Trucost in the preparation of the Puma and Kering EP&L analyses, is one of those offering semiproprietary methodologies. In what it dubs its TIMM (Total Impact Measurement and Management) approach, PwC adds a fourth element to the triple bottom line—tax. The idea here is to identify and measure a business's overall tax contribution. Recent controversies spotlighting the tax system manipulations practiced by companies like Apple, Google, and Starbucks have underscored the increasing importance of this area.[8] Significantly, one key characteristic of the TIMM approach (and, one hopes, of other future accounting methods) is that it aims to be both backward- and forward-looking.

Those leading such experiments often argue, as does PwC, that it is too early to regulate for multidimensional accounting. The B Team leaders, most of whom are experimenting in this area, agree. However, the main thrust of Plan B is that no amount of toe-dipping is going to crack the Breakthrough Challenge. Something more is needed—and broader changes in accountancy suggest that accountants are going to have to mutate and evolve at unprecedented speed in the coming decade.

The International Integrated Reporting Council (IIRC) is at the forefront of a new system of corporate reporting, central to which is a global framework that supports an organization's efforts to communicate value, its business model, and interconnections between the various "capitals" used to deliver its strategy. "The move toward greater corporate transparency is a supertrend," argues IIRC CEO Paul Druckman. But there are wider considerations to take into account here. Druckman notes,

> The risk is that this trend leads to the production of more data and information, disconnected from the strategy and value drivers that are central to effective operation of capital markets. The primary purpose of an integrated report is to equip providers of financial capital with the information they need to allocate capital efficiently

and productively. What integrated reporting reveals is the underlying resilience of the business model, the strategy and how the business creates value over time. Our main priority is to bring about the early adoption of integrated reporting by working with businesses and investors, encouraging market innovation and removing any regulatory barriers.

Organizations like the IIRC are talking to businesses and governments about transparency, reporting, and accounting. Governments and business must work together to encourage business to radically improve its accounting and reporting. For example, the APEC Business Advisory Council, which reports directly to the twenty-three finance ministries in the APEC member communities, recently noted that it sees government moving toward a significantly more important role in this space, not least when it comes to offering strategic endorsement to integrated reporting as a way of contributing to greater financial stability and sustainability.

Critically, too, government must also ensure that the resulting flows of data, information, and intelligence are themselves integrated in ways that make system conditions much more transparent to business leaders, investors, customers, and consumers.

Other Initiatives

New initiatives are evolving that promise to track and account for the wider environmental, social, and governance effects of what companies are doing. One example is the Energy Points initiative, which uses no less than 1.8 billion conversion factors to translate various different energy units—for example, mBTUs and kilowatt-hours—into an Energy Point, which is defined as being equivalent to one gallon of gasoline, and allows accurate comparisons of energy costs.[9] For example, a kilowatt-hour produced by a coal-burning power plant has a different carbon intensity than one powered by natural gas or wind farms. A gallon of water supplied in the Northeast of America requires less energy to deliver than a gallon does in the Southwest.

Energy Points is just one initiative among many in this space, with huge potential for convergence and consolidation. The Carbon Disclosure Project, an international nonprofit organization, provides a global framework within which companies and cities alike can measure, disclose, manage, and share vital information related to climate change and, increasingly, water security. The organization is also helping persuade a growing number of companies and analysts of the importance of factoring carbon (and water) costs into their routine calculations, so that more and more of the data will actually be used.

There are many other forms of supply chain transparency. Levi's, for example, recently launched its Wellthread Dockers, a line of what were promptly dubbed "triple bottom line khakis"[10] because they documented supply chains and externalities reaching back into countries like Bangladesh, Cambodia, Pakistan, and Egypt. Like every other product we buy and use, each pair of jeans or chinos is trailed by a wake of ethical, social, and environmental issues, most of them invisible to the consumer's eye.

Breakthrough leaders must measure the social, economic, and environmental costs of their businesses — both within their own walls and throughout their supply chains and value webs. They must use and help coevolve these new, systemwide tools that will allow them to measure and manage the true costs of doing business. They also know that applying true accounting principles requires them to partner with governments and other organizations in order to reach new levels of transparency, while simultaneously measuring and accounting for the effectiveness of those governments.

Mo Ibrahim, founder of Celtel and a B Team member, launched the Ibrahim Index of African Governance in 2007, a comprehensive collection of quantitative data on governance in Africa that helps citizens, governments, and business assess the delivery of public goods and services, as well as policy outcomes.[11] Most CEOs are not democratically elected to serve the public interest, so we need politicians and policymakers to help power and steer the necessary transformations. To celebrate those who do, Ibrahim also founded a prize for achievement in African leadership, whose laureates lifted their people out of poverty and created breakthrough initiatives for equitable and sustainable prosperity.[12]

○   ○   ○

It is often said that modern accounting is, at best, akin to looking in the rearview mirror, tracking where a business has been and some of the key things that have happened along the way. If the discipline is to survive and thrive, it will need to learn how to look forward—and how to capture both social and environmental risks and opportunities. As this work proceeds, the breakthrough leaders now working toward defining tomorrow's bottom line know that they must also find new ways to calculate true returns. We'll look at that challenge—and at the need to reboot economics—next, in Chapter Four.

4

Calculate True Returns

Business exists to create returns, usually in the form of revenues, profits, and dividends. As accountants harvest the relevant financial numbers, business leaders, financial analysts, and investors use them to track and guide the performance of a given business. Economists then use the information to determine whether, collectively, we are going up or down, forward or backward. This is important work, but the apparent obsession of most economists with a single measure for success, gross domestic product (GDP), began to look even more threadbare as the Great Recession hit its stride in 2008.

"Economists were like medieval priests who had a special relationship with God and spoke in Latin to the average punter, and said, 'This is way above your head. Don't worry about it,'" notes Irish economist David McWilliams, founder of an economics summit in Kilkenny that brings together mainstream economists with comedians to present economics topics in a more understandable fashion. The downturn, McWilliams recalls, ensured that "the Irish discovered that most economists, and everyone else who ran their country (or other countries), had no idea what they were talking about."

It is increasingly clear that economics, the master discipline of capitalism, is in dire need of a fundamental reboot as part of the effort to calculate the true returns of business and our economies. There have been various efforts to calculate the "true" or "real" rate of return for given businesses—for example, by ensuring that the prevailing rates of inflation are taken into account. What we need here, in addition, is the progressive factoring in of the costs—and value—of the wider economic, social, and environmental impacts of a business. Before we get into the practicalities of how true returns are best calculated and of how the discipline of economics might evolve, let's briefly consider what exactly it is that economists do.

o Rebooting Economics

In simple terms, we are told, economists "study how society distributes resources, such as land, labor, raw materials, and machinery, to produce goods and services. They conduct research, collect and analyze data, monitor economic trends, and develop forecasts on a wide variety of issues, including energy costs, inflation, interest rates, exchange rates, business cycles, taxes, and employment levels, among others."[1] These activities are helpful, indeed indispensable to the functioning of business and a modern economy. But if our economic tools are flawed, and if our economists and corporate dashboards are giving us the wrong information, we risk steering off the road as we try to travel the winding route to sustainability.

The challenge is made more complicated by the fact that many leaders, much of the time, operate within economic realities (some would argue myths) that potentially blind them to key aspects of the wider reality. "We live in an economic myth the way the fish swim in the sea: unconsciously," explains Betty Sue Flowers, an emeritus professor at the University of Texas who has studied myth making. "The economic myth is not synonymous with capitalism, [but the different] varieties of capitalism are its hardiest expressions."

Economics, like accounting, remains both monocular and myopic. It is too inclined to focus on anything to do with money, and to discount away a wide range of nonfinancial factors—or, perhaps it would be more accurate to say, factors that have not yet been expressed in financial form. Traditional economic theory encourages us to focus on financial forms of capital and to ignore other forms, among them human, intellectual, social, and natural capital.

A key issue, both in economics and in accounting, is where to draw the line. Since the environmental revolution began in the early 1960s, business has been encouraged to draw the line of responsibility and accountability progressively farther afield, right out to and including the oceans (with the loss of oceanic fisheries), the stratospheric ozone layer (which has been damaged by CFCs and other ozone-depleting substances), and the planet's entire biosphere (because of species loss and climate change).

One of the most important things tomorrow's business leaders can do in the short term is to speak out about the weaknesses of much of today's economic thinking. Breakthrough leaders find ways to encourage and reward the efforts of those who are trying to shift economics onto a new footing. We must track down, engage with, and support those who are reinventing the discipline. If we are to inject enough capital into new forms of conscious, regenerative, sustainable capitalism, we will have no choice but to factor in the true cost of doing business. However, for us to move beyond—or radically improve—measures like GDP, we must learn to see our economies, value webs, and businesses as actors in a much wider set of dynamic processes.

Among related efforts is the work of organizations like TEEB (The Economics of Ecosystems and Biodiversity) and individuals like economist Jeffrey D. Sachs. Sachs is the Quetelet Professor of Sustainable Development and professor of health policy and management at Columbia University. He also serves as director of the Earth Institute, an organization that works to address such global issues as climate change, environmental degradation, and sustainability. Sachs and the team at the Earth Institute understand that economics, society, and environment are inextricably linked and that when the true costs of doing business are factored in, dramatic new opportunities can be created. Sachs explains that "since the 2008 financial crash, our country has been reeling without getting its economic policy right. What we needed then, and need now, is a new kind of macroeconomics; one that aims for investment-led growth, not consumption-led growth."[2]

The B Team concludes that we must ensure that the discipline of economics evolves to make it fit for the emerging—and very different—realities of the twenty-first century. This requires not just the application and further refinement of tomorrow's accounting principles, which we discussed in Chapter Three, but also the measurement of the true cost of business activities and the true returns produced in the process. Happily, this does not mean that we must wait for decades until the discipline of economics is turned upside down and inside out. The process is already under way. To paraphrase science fiction author William Gibson, the future [of Economics] is already here—it's just not evenly distributed. Yet.

○ Getting a Grip on Externalities

We must revisit how we see and measure the importance of items that are currently accounted for as externalities. These are the costs imposed and, to some extent, the wider benefits provided beyond the boundaries of a given business, at least as defined by economists and accountants. Among the negative externalities that a business may cause are noise and water pollution; moral hazards associated with smoking, drug, and alcohol abuse, as well as bribery and corruption; deforestation, soil loss, and overfishing; and the production of toxins and radioactive waste.

As some of those externalities come home to roost, investors and businesses will increasingly find themselves left with what are called "stranded assets." These are assets that have become obsolete and are no longer able to generate the sort of financial returns investors expected when they put their money in. For example, consider the fate of the brand-new Spiritwood lignite plant in Minnesota. When the U.S. Environmental Protection Agency raised its mercury emission standards, increasing the costs of producing electricity from coal, the plant was mothballed before it had even started supplying electricity. The plant may well reopen at a later time, but the implication was not lost on forward-thinking investors. We must work to ensure that our global, national, and corporate balance sheets record such stranded assets as potential losses — and to avoid creating the next generation of strandable assets.

One key challenge in accounting for externalities is that organizations tend to track the benefits — at least as far as they flow to the main actors involved — without tracking many of the costs. Negative externalities are often overlooked, and must be addressed, but it is worth noting that there has also been growing interest in positive externalities. These are costs or benefits for which enterprises are not directly rewarded. Infosys in India, for example, is seen to have produced major positive externalities through training generations of information and communications technology (ICT) specialists who have gone on to evolve the country's ICT sector. It is entirely proper that business leaders should try to capture such benefits, but we should be watchful for efforts to use such arguments as a form of greenwashing, in an attempt to offset and excuse the very real negative impacts of a particular business or industry.

Measuring true returns requires organizations of every ilk to include in their bottom-line computations the cost of negative externalities, as a minimum. Whether called true cost accounting or full cost accounting, this is the process of measuring and accounting for the full costs of doing business, within the core operations of an organization and throughout its supply chain and value webs, and—ultimately—in the wider world.

Richard Mattison, CEO of Trucost, has spent more than a decade examining the economic consequences of business activity and practices. One of the industries he has investigated is information technology. He notes that the production of personal computers is just one example of a business whose costs are consistently underreported. He points out that if externalities were fully accounted for, the true cost of a desktop computer would be around 14 percent higher than its retail price, and a laptop would be 6 percent more expensive. Why? Because most PC makers fail to factor in the costs of raw material processing, manufacturing, transportation, end disposal, recycling, carbon emissions, water, and waste flows.[3]

Water, for example, is largely ignored as a cost, even though its consumption can have major economic consequences. According to new research by Trucost for the TEEB for Business Coalition, the unpaid environmental cost of water consumption by global primary production and processing business sectors is $1.9 trillion—or around 2.5 percent of GDP.[4] Corn, cotton, rice, and wheat farming are among the industries with the highest impact on water consumption. These costs can have lasting and important ramifications far beyond farms and fields. Volatile cotton prices, for example, have prompted a number of retailers—among them

Adidas, American Eagle Outfitters, Gap, and H&M—to issue profit warnings.

Entire library shelves of books have been written about the importance of water and the role it plays in the global economy. Too many of us don't give water a second thought—we turn on the tap, and it pours out. In many parts of the world, however, demand is outpacing supply, with water scarcity and security emerging as issues at the core of tomorrow's geopolitical agenda.

The demand for action is growing. In 2008, for example, business leaders at the World Economic Forum Annual Meeting issued a Call to Action on Water, "to raise awareness and develop a better understanding of how water is linked to economic growth across a nexus of issues and to make clear the water security challenge we face if a business as usual approach to water management is maintained."[5] In a report on the water-energy-food nexus, the World Economic Forum Water Initiative noted that "there is a structural problem in how we manage water across the web of our global economy. Unless it is checked, worsening water security will soon tear into various parts of the global economic system."[6]

Water is but one issue—one aspect of our resource consumption—that requires both measurement and management. Other externalities are already having an impact on the true returns produced by businesses and economies alike. As a result, calculating the true cost of doing business or operating an economy is going to require extraordinary levels of collaboration across nations, sectors, and functions.

Breakthrough leaders aiming to measure the full impact of their business practices must engage a wider world of experts and stakeholders to make sure they get this right. That may mean that CEOs and chief financial officers (CFOs) have to surrender a certain degree of control and allow other C-suite executives, such as chief sustainability officers, to get involved. It also is likely to mean that organizations must reconsider the accounting processes and tools they use. It is worth noting that in some cases, internalizing the full costs of a company's or an industry's operations may blow the current business model out of the water.

This was true, for example, of industries producing asbestos and CFCs. Today, coal mining and coal-fired power industries are in the same position. If, for example, they were forced to take on the full costs of the public health problems and climate destabilization for which they are (and are likely to be) responsible, the economics of their operations would implode. Indeed, there are signs that this is now beginning to happen in places like the United States and Germany, as coal-fired power stations are caught between the opposing pressures of climate campaigners and the burgeoning renewable energy industry.

Already the forces of creative destruction are tearing into the economics of power generation — and the fortunes of some of Europe's biggest energy utilities. At their peak in 2008, the top energy utilities were worth an estimated €1 trillion ($1.3 trillion). By 2013, they were worth less than half that.[7] Unfortunately, when these upheavals occur, they also tend to damage the interests of employees, communities, financial institutions, and those with pension policies.

Directly or indirectly, some renewable energy organizations are beginning to factor into their progress metrics the benefits of knocking out increasingly large slices of the climate-destabilizing fossil fuels sector. Despite the inevitable teething problems, the impact of calculating true returns could be strongly beneficial, showing how industries and companies can create new forms of value over time, including a range of positive externalities.

o Engaging the Global C-Suite

Growing numbers of executives across the global C-suite are waking up to the need to expand the scope of their accounting processes, but CFOs have been lagging behind the curve. A report titled *Future Proofed Decision Making* produced by Accounting for Sustainability (A4S) opens with quotations from two leading CFOs.[8] "It is difficult for accountants and engineers to deal with these nebulous things," was how one summed up the problem. "If money goes out the door, I am interested," said the second. "If it is a notional cost to society, I am not." Such people, as yet, are not interested in true costs and true returns. They aim to focus on what the financial markets currently want them to do.

Despite such entrenched mind-sets, we have seen considerable progress in recent times. As Mark Goyder, founder director of Tomorrow's Company, recalls, "Fifteen years ago, Stuart Hampson, our second chairman and then chair of John Lewis [the U.K. retailer], used to say that we will know we are succeeding when we find more finance directors [FDs] in our projects and at our events. This is now happening, and we find ourselves dealing with FDs who understand the close connection between sustainability and efficient resource use, and want to see this reported holistically and effectively."

Even more positively, the A4S report noted that "the translation of environmental and social impacts into the language of accountancy is a rapidly evolving area." As a result, it concluded, CFOs and their colleagues will soon have "a more complete view of the true costs and benefits of an organization's activities," enabling them to get a better grip on the relevant risks and opportunities.

A growing number of business leaders are attempting to accelerate the process of engaging the C-suite by appointing chief sustainability officers (CSOs). The CSO trend is both a symptom of the pressures now building on business and an increasingly important vector of change in its own right. Often considered the first person to take on the title, Linda Fisher is vice president and CSO at E. I. DuPont de Nemours and Company; she assumed the CSO position in 2004. At the time, DuPont had been having considerable success reducing its environmental footprint, particularly when it came to reducing greenhouse gas and improving energy efficiency, but challenges remained, such as tackling resistance from leaders who questioned the very need for the CSO role.

"A key challenge has been convincing business leaders that sustainability issues are not 'fads,' and that to be successful long term, these issues need to be central to their strategies," she says. "On the opposite side of the coin, it has been rewarding to see business leaders develop a growing awareness that developing products that make our customers more sustainable is a great growth strategy." To embed this sort of thinking, CSOs can help CFOs and other C-suite colleagues to manage and measure the performance of the business in very different ways.

Although CSOs do help engage the C-suite, the ultimate goal must still be a broad commitment from all executives. "The C-suite should be a team of sustainability champions that understands both the challenges and the business opportunities — a team that knows how to communicate and cooperate with government, NGOs, and social networks," says Natura cofounder and board member Guilherme Leal, a member of The B Team. "The number-one CSO should be the CEO."

Peter Bakker, president of the World Business Council for Sustainable Development (WBCSD) and a former CFO at TNT, echoes this view: "We should strive for a situation where the board as a whole and not just a separate CSR or CSO officer feels responsible, and where decision making tools like the environmental profit and loss and social profit and loss approaches are reflected into rule-based integrated reporting systems. In this world of integrated thinking, the CFO becomes responsible for all forms of capital, not just financial capital."

o Investing for True Returns

The B Team leaders see an urgent need for new forms of return on investment (ROI) to be developed and mainstreamed. They encourage the development of financial methods and institutions that aim to get a better sense of the performance of particular sectors and companies against multiple bottom lines.

The sort of institutions they have in mind include Generation Investment Management, a private, independent investment management firm founded by former U.S. vice president Al Gore and David Blood, former head of Goldman Sachs Asset Management. Founded in 2004, Generation is built around the "idea that sustainability factors — economic, environmental, social and governance criteria — will drive a company's returns over the long term."[9] The firm's analysts integrate sustainability research into their equity analysis, focusing on "key drivers of global change, including climate change and environmental degradation; poverty and development; water and natural resource scarcity; pandemics and healthcare; and demographics, migration, and urbanization."

These drivers are crucial issues to consider when computing the true returns of a given business. Interestingly, the Generation team is trying to work out how to change the incentive structures that help sustain problem industries. "The urgency now means we have a very short time to make a dent in this," Blood explains. "The card we can play is that from a risk management perspective, it is so logical for business, investors, and economies to take the next steps. The costs of inaction for a pension fund are just too severe."

The Generation team also concludes that there is a growing need to incentivize and reward long-term investing, and the firm has been investigating the field of "loyalty-driven securities" (see Chapter Ten). The logic here is that "the dominance of short-termism in the market fosters general market instability and undermines the efforts of executives seeking long-term value creation," as Blood puts it. "The common argument that more liquidity is always better for markets is based on long-discredited elements of the now-obsolete 'standard model' of economics, including the illusion of perfect information and the assumption that markets tend toward equilibrium."

To counter short-termism, such leaders are concluding that companies will need to issue securities that offer investors financial rewards for holding on to shares for a certain number of years. Although Generation's research on the feasibility of so-called L-Shares (discussed in Chapter Ten) revealed limited support for the adoption of such financial instruments, a clear consensus emerged in favor of continued investigation of other mechanisms to grow the pool of patient capital.

As The B Team pushes toward the objectives of Plan B, we see the rise of new communities and movements that are committed to funding high-potential ventures in this space, both old and new. Among these movements are the rapidly evolving fields of venture philanthropy and philanthrocapitalism, both of which involve high-net-worth individuals and families who invest in high-impact social ventures.

This trend has been most pronounced in North America, where people like Bill and Melinda Gates, Warren Buffett, Jeff Skoll, and Pierre Omidyar have applied skills learned during the New Economy era to the fast-paced world of social enterprise — including mutated forms of concepts like replication and scaling. New initiatives also have emerged to track, coordinate, and support all this effort, including the Global Impact Investment Network (GIIN), which is dedicated to increasing the scale and effectiveness of impact investing.

Impact investments are those made into companies, organizations, and funds with the intention of generating measurable positive social and environmental impact alongside a financial return.[10] The efforts of impact investors and social entrepreneurs are likely to be insufficient on their own, however. In embracing the Breakthrough Challenge, we need new forms of alliance between business, investors, governments, public institutions, and civil society organizations.

The key, argues Sally Osberg, president and CEO of the Skoll Foundation, is partnering with new types of actors to boost the chances of replication and scaling. As she explains, "The most successful social entrepreneurs in the Skoll portfolio — that is, those who have achieved the greatest impact — have created and continue to manage substantive partnerships with public and private sector entities." This also holds true in sectors like microfinance and crowdfunding, which help get money where normal funders cannot yet reach.

The real challenge will be to shift mainstream finance. B Team adviser John Fullerton, a former managing director at JP Morgan and now president of the Capital Institute, notes that "mainstream finance has two problems making it hard for those involved to 'see' this shift. First, they are under assault and overwhelmed with immediate crisis management, as a result of the financial crisis. Their very identity is at stake. A lot of fear tied to ego. Second, finance, being highly abstract and reductionist, has the hardest time seeing the world holistically. As a result, there is great ignorance within the financial sector. Combined, this reality poses a great systemic risk to society, more so than too-big-to-fail banks. Literally."

That's not to say that everything about capitalism is all bad, Fullerton notes. "Modern financial capitalism has many good qualities that should be retained, and many destructive qualities that must be legislated and regulated away. However, we must also recognize that the core objective of optimizing financial return on capital investment (in the relatively short term) that defines today's economic system is simply not up to the task of our increasingly complex world."

○ Scaling Societal Value

Measuring the true cost and returns of business will require rethinking everything from the cost of resources to the pricing of intangibles. More immediately, it is likely to require leaders to find ways to replicate and scale initiatives that are successful in very different organizations and sectors. That is one reason why we increasingly see mainstream businesses reaching out to leading social innovators, entrepreneurs, and investors, to learn from their successes (and failures) in tackling challenges that are now pushing into the mainstream agenda.

Some key players admit, however, that they are nervous about the current obsession with scaling, at least when applied too eagerly to the world of social innovation. Indeed, Sally Osberg questions the whole notion. "I recoil at the shibboleth in our space about 'scaling' based on the belief that the only scale that matters is the scale of the organization," she explains. "Our experience suggests that an organization's budget, the size of its staff, or the number of offices have little to do with what matters most."

She offers a striking example, noting that "Partners in Health was a relatively small, albeit definitely scrappy and ambitious organization, when it took up the gauntlet of proving that complex drug regimens could be successfully delivered with community health workers, and that multi-drug-resistant TB could be successfully treated and contained. Ultimately, it achieved better results in the shanty towns of Lima than were being recorded in cities like New York."

That said, given the nature and dimensions of the Breakthrough Challenge, the principle of scaling must remain a key part of our thinking. Used in the right way, it also should increasingly inform and guide the work of impact investors, entrepreneurs and intrapreneurs, major corporations, and government policymakers alike.

The efforts of major philanthropists have helped shape the thinking of the new generation of impact investors—and their work, in turn, will progressively influence mainstream players. Long before the mainstream financial markets wake up, though, the likelihood is that the businesses that get this right will see growing benefits in such areas as talent recruitment and retention, customer and consumer loyalty, and brand equity and reputation. In response, an increasing proportion of financial analysts will embrace at least some measures of such forms of intangible value in their calculations.

o   o   o

If we are to build a more sustainable future around the people-planet-profit agenda, then we must look much more closely at the true costs of doing business and explore new ways of creating shared value across both socioeconomic and generational divides. We must adopt new and improved accounting principles and methods, and embark on the transformation of the master discipline of economics. We also must work out how to create both old and new forms of well-being at the levels of the individual, the community, the nation, and, ultimately, the global biosphere. We'll look at that next, in Chapter Five.

5

Embrace Well-Being

If you are unlucky enough to suffer from an anxiety disorder, depression, or autism, but lucky enough to live in Dorset, England, you may find that the local doctor is willing to prescribe a free surfing course as part of a program sponsored by the country's National Health Service. The idea here is not simply to treat such complaints with drugs but to help those affected to break out of the destructive spirals that such disorders can promote. The results so far suggest that those who have gone through such a course experience improvements in confidence, self-esteem, and well-being.[1]

You could say that Patagonia founder and owner Yvon Chouinard was well ahead of this wave with his book *Let My People Go Surfing*.[2] Subtitled *The Education of a Reluctant Businessman*, this was an early example of a business leader making the connection between corporate citizenship, environmental sustainability, and people's well-being. The ripples continue to spread.

There is a growing recognition that business must become a primary driver of holistic well-being, adding multiple forms of value through new types of wealth creation that respect human rights and ensure new forms of employee welfare, health care, and citizen engagement. At the same time, business leaders need to reduce impacts on the environment to ensure the survival and well-being of future generations.

Although many leaders continue to see well-being as an economic intangible that has little to do with earnings and profits, The B Team leaders see it as central to business success, both today and tomorrow. Arianna Huffington, for example, notes that the cost of stress to American businesses is as much as $300 billion annually, which is why about 35 percent of all large and midsize U.S. businesses now offer some sort of stress-reduction program.

"Less-stressed and healthier employees are more creative, more effective, and less likely to get sick, which in the long run also reduces health insurance costs for employers," she says. "Businesses that drive increases in social well-being also have better standing with consumers and are better positioned to secure trust in their brands. Increasing well-being drives positive sentiment and builds business confidence, which in turn support economic development and growth."

○ Positioning Business as a Driver of Well-Being

It is time for many more business leaders to step up and embrace the benefits of promoting well-being for their customers, employees, and communities. At the most basic level, of course, business creates various forms of economic activity, wealth creation, and growth. All of these help promote well-being, though the upsides are too often undermined by the negative externalities that are still ignored in traditional balance sheets.

Leaders who have embraced the well-being agenda have done so because they understand that conventional measures of financial performance or economic growth may miss critical risk factors if they are too short-term oriented. They also know that they must look at well-being not just in terms of their own employees but also throughout their supply chains. Well-being begins with the people who make, grow, and harvest raw materials, and it continues with those who produce finished goods and those who sell them, before shifting to the consumers who put products and services to use. It doesn't end there, however. If the relevant operations and activities draw down natural resources, leave toxins in the environment, or pump greenhouse gases into the atmosphere, to take just a few examples, some of the negative impacts can damage well-being over decades or even generations.

The B Team leaders argue that well-managed organizations with healthier supply chains will do better as businesses in the long run. Those that fail to consider the well-being of their entire organization, their supply chains, and their value webs will find it impossible to tap into the full potential of all their key stakeholders—risking the loss of their license to operate, innovate, and lead. So it's time for business leaders to embrace well-being in the broadest meaning of the word.

B Team leaders like Huffington and Shari Arison, owner of the Arison Group, a global business and philanthropic organization working to improve lives worldwide through values-based investments, underscore the importance of healthy workplace conditions and safe working practices in enhancing the well-being of all employees—in terms of their physical, mental, and spiritual health. Such leaders argue that the masculine, testosterone-fueled forms of capitalism that have driven so much of our economic development since the Industrial Revolution are also a root cause of many of our wider social and environmental ills. But whereas traditional business leaders have been happy to set those ills aside as externalities, many clean technology and social innovators now see major opportunities for change and aim to confront these problems head-on.

Gary Cohen is founder, president, and executive director of Health Care Without Harm, the international coalition for environmentally responsible health care. His central idea has been that the health care sector, operating with the Hippocratic imperative "First, do no harm," should be the leading sector in ending our reliance on fossil fuels, toxic chemicals, and industrial agriculture.

It is no longer simply a question of people being concerned about personal health and well-being but of using the potential leverage that the health care industry can offer to drive positive change. Cohen explains that "the health care sector, which is approaching 20 percent of GDP in the U.S. and 10 percent globally, has enough power and the right mission to countervail against the fossil fuel and chemical industries. We concluded that if we brought the latest science linking the environment and public health to the sector, they would become engaged in transforming their practices and their supply chains."

Cohen and Health Care Without Harm have worked hard to change health care in positive ways. Their efforts have helped drive the elimination in the United States of medical equipment that contains mercury, and they succeeded in winning a global treaty that completely phases out mercury in health care by 2020. In addition, they have closed more than forty-five hundred medical waste incinerators, demonstrating that hospitals can reduce waste, utilize alternative treatment technologies, and save money. In the process, they have helped create a $500 million market for reprocessed medical devices, saving hospitals hundreds of millions of dollars. They codeveloped a building tool called the Green Guide for Healthcare and have worked with 265 hospital projects, representing 40 million square feet, to utilize this approach. They also have worked with the U.S. Green Building Council to embed the relevant mind-sets and standards into the LEED standard for the health care sector.

The efforts and initiatives that Cohen and Health Care Without Harm have undertaken provide just a few, but powerfully concrete, examples of the benefits of embracing well-being throughout an organization, its supply chains, and its industry. Not only are the financial benefits compelling, but so are the related intangibles, involving contributions in areas like health, consumer confidence, and overall welfare. The challenge here will be to find new ways to measure those benefits — real and intangible — and to incentivize and reward those organizations that deliver them.

○ Measuring — and Valuing — Happiness and Well-Being

As society becomes more interested in well-being, economists, business leaders, and governments are looking for better ways to measure it. Governments in the United States and Britain,[3] among others, are launching happiness and well-being indexes of their own, further testament to the interest in measuring factors that many would consider intangible, vague, and subjective.

The message is clear: valuing and measuring happiness and well-being is a crucial task for breakthrough leaders. Indeed, in the future, those businesses that embrace the Breakthrough Challenge will measure their success in part by the state of well-being, happiness, wisdom, and service in their organizations, their supply chains, and their value webs. Doing so will require new models, different approaches, fresh strategies, and creative indexes.

The B Team expects that a growing number of experiments in this area will lead to an expanding range of new models that can be tested, consolidated, scaled, and replicated.

Standard Chartered, the multinational banking and financial services group, for example, is one of those pioneering a new index, in this case the Standard Chartered Development Index, or SCDI, which measures changes in five aspects of sustainable growth.[4] The original work was led by the firm's head of macro-economic research, a former chief economist. What is striking is how prominent a role health and well-being now play in such assessments.

The five dimensions of progress in the index are GDP per capita, years of education, life expectancy, environmental health (for example, air and water quality), and "ecosystem vitality," a measure of longer-term sustainability, including the potential impact of climate change. The top performers in the first version of the index, measuring progress between 2000 and 2012, were Ghana, Uganda, Korea, Bangladesh, Singapore, Egypt, Nigeria, India, Brazil, and Indonesia. The reason for these perhaps surprising results is that the index is designed to be an indicator of progress rather than a static ranking.

The emerging countries in the thirty-one-country sample were more likely to have seen significant progress as their economies grew than were developed countries. That said, most emerging countries show declining scores in terms of ecosystem vitality. China, despite its stellar GDP growth in recent years, coupled with improvements in education, appeared farther down the list, reflecting weak scores on life expectancy, environmental health, and ecosystem vitality. Such factors increasingly shape the competitiveness of cities, regions, and nations.

The Global Competitiveness Index (GCI) helps countries improve the economic dimension of their development strategies, but such strategies are incomplete if they do not look at social and environmental value creation. Hence the idea of a Social Progress Index. "The idea went through two key changes," explains Michael Green, who heads the Social Progress Imperative. "First, it was agreed to create two indices: the Social Progress Index (measuring outcomes) and the Social Progress Capacity Index (measuring inputs). And, second, it was decided to base the Social Progress

Index entirely on social and environmental indicators—which will allow us to interrogate the relationship between economic development (measured in terms of GDP) and social progress more rigorously over time."

All of this links to the challenge of changing the way that countries and business calculate the bottom line. "I think that it has to include some way of accounting for the impact of net greenhouse gas emissions, given the urgency and gravity of the threat of climate change," Green says. "The Social Progress Index quite effectively captures the way that environmental sustainability is negatively correlated with rising GDP in general, reflected in the deceleration in aggregate social progress scores as countries reach high levels of income, with lower scores for the more energy-intensive countries."

Communities also are finding ways to successfully measure happiness and well-being, understanding that satisfied residents can bring value to towns large and small. In the United States, cities in Vermont, Washington, and Wisconsin have surveyed residents to gauge their happiness—efforts that have helped them understand where they can make meaningful improvements.[5] Seattle, for example, recently launched the Happiness Initiative, "a national project designed to transform communities by using measures of civic success and well-being in place of traditional economic measures."[6]

Although there may be reasons to be skeptical about the need to measure factors like happiness—with some even speaking of an "index mania"—other commentators support the measurement of happiness and well-being. For example, organizations like the United Nations, Gallup, and the Skoll Foundation consider happiness a key issue and are investigating ways to measure it as a step toward improving social and economic development in countries the world over.[7]

The trend is likely to build. Indeed, the tempo of index launches is accelerating. In 2012, economists at the Organization for Economic Cooperation and Development (OECD) told a large audience in Paris that they hoped their Better Life Index — launched a year previously — "would persuade governments to focus as much on factors like environment and community cohesiveness, as on GDP measurements like productivity and income."[8]

We can count on a growing number of communities, corporations, cities, and governments around the world to invest significant time, effort, and resources in finding new ways to measure, value, and manage happiness and well-being. In the process, we will discover that although in many ways such issues and outcomes may remain subjective and intangible, they are increasingly quantifiable.

New tools are emerging to help citizens measure key aspects of their environment and others health risk factors. Take TellSpec, a new product that uses a spectrometer to identify potential toxins in food and relays them to a mobile phone app that converts the information into risk factors and health advice.[9] This is likely just the beginning, as a growing number of entrepreneurs and intrapreneurs are working toward change in related areas.

Leading corporations also are coming around to this way of thinking. In a report titled *Wellbeing at Work*, the U.K.-based Institute of Directors, Standard Life Healthcare, the Department for Work and Pensions (DWP), and the Health and Safety Executive (HSE) argue that managing well-being in the workplace can boost both individual and corporate performance. Improving well-being, health, and safety results in reduced accident claims, absenteeism, and work-related injuries as well as increased productivity and improved employee-client relationships. Better morale, lower turnover, and an enriched corporate reputation also result from efforts to improve well-being.[10]

Tracking and valuing happiness and well-being may seem a tricky task, but there are a growing number of tools to help us do this, ranging from simple measures of absenteeism, to surveys designed to monitor stress and job satisfaction, to online health profiles.

In case this sounds complicated or expensive (or both), relax. Experience suggests that many organizations do not immediately need to institute complicated well-being plans or offer expensive benefits in order to improve the health and well-being of their employees. Often something as simple as, say, directly addressing absenteeism with individual employees can be enough to improve overall morale. Coaching, monitoring workloads, and rewarding employees for outstanding performance are other simple ways that can help improve individual well-being. Ensuring that an organization's purpose clearly aligns with that of wider society also can boost employees' sense of fulfillment.

Breakthrough leaders understand that all forms of well-being are interconnected. That said, some will have to learn this lesson the hard way, and many will find it a stretch to find effective ways to measure well-being. As with other challenges, it will be difficult for any single company to solve these problems on its own. Instead, organizations and their leaders will need to align with other actors trying to shape and drive the health and well-being agenda. It will become commonplace, for example, that leaders who can embrace some aspects of the health and well-being agenda also are likely to be able to embrace other dimensions as well, signaling the sort of leadership mind-set that will attract, motivate, and retain tomorrow's talent.

o Taking a Cue from Social Entrepreneurs

Social entrepreneurs are increasingly celebrated, as are social intrapreneurs — innovators and change agents working within companies and other organizations, sometimes in alliance with social entrepreneurs, all with the aim of creating new forms of environmental, social, and governance (ESG) value.[11] Whether they are working on financial, social, or environmental improvements, they are all focusing on various forms of well-being.

When we say "well-being" here, we include civil rights, human rights, and, even further out, animal rights. We include greater access for poorer people to such things as medicines, finance, renewable energy, and clean water. We also include efforts to promote improvements in work-life balance.

One key factor behind the growing interest in the world of social enterprise is that mainstream business leaders increasingly understand that social entrepreneurs set out from the get-go to improve the well-being of people and planet. These extraordinary change-makers establish initiatives or enterprises with the purpose of driving social change in some way. By virtue of what they do, their organizations blur the lines between "business" and "cause."[12]

Muhammad Yunus has successfully—and repeatedly— blurred these boundaries. He points to broadening areas of overlap between social entrepreneurism and the agendas of mainstream business leaders. In recent years, and alongside the late C. K. Prahalad, he has emerged as a globally celebrated champion of the idea that, wherever you look, there are vast markets and economic opportunities, for the poor as well as the rich, lying untapped at the bottom of the wealth pyramid. As founder of the widely celebrated Grameen Bank, for example, he developed the concept of microfinance.

"Social business is about solving human problems," he explains, "all kinds of human problems—energy, planet, health issues, social issues. The essence is that the challenge can't be addressed by making it exclusively personal-benefit driven. Personal interest has to be set within a broader framework that includes both the personal and the social. A key step is to recognize that anything affecting our planet is ultimately a human problem. We see the environment as a strong part of social business."

Organizations like the Skoll Foundation also are working in ways small and large to improve the well-being of people around the world. The foundation focuses on providing economic, educational, and employment opportunities designed to improve well-being and enhance personal dignity.[13] It works with a variety of pioneering organizations the world over, including Aflatoun, which helps children "learn about themselves, child rights, saving, basic financial concepts, and enterprise"; Manchester Bidwell Corporation, a vocational training program; and YouthBuild USA, which "teaches at-risk young people to construct homes and offers at-risk youth leadership training, education, and skills that lead to good jobs."[14]

Worldwide, social enterprises are working to improve well-being in a mind-boggling number of ways. Some, like Grameen Bank, the Skoll Foundation, the Omidyar Foundation, and the Bill & Melinda Gates Foundation, are chipping away at large, global issues by working with partners to tackle challenges that many see as impossible to solve. Just one example from the Gates portfolio is the foundation's efforts to eradicate such diseases as polio and malaria.

Others, like Wellbeing Enterprises, are working at a local level to improve the quality of life of communities. Based in the United Kingdom, Wellbeing Enterprises provides a variety of community-based programs designed to improve mental well-being, including self-help groups, training sessions, and educational programs.[15]

Although improving happiness and well-being is a key tenet of Plan B, this doesn't mean that breakthrough leaders necessarily must focus on solving huge, global problems through complex programs with enormous scope. The B Team leaders would instead encourage like-minded leaders and their organizations to begin by harnessing the resources of social intrapreneurs both inside the organization and in other organizations, and also the imagination, ambition, and energies of social entrepreneurs who have begun to work out how some of our greatest challenges can be cracked.

In some cases, the best way forward for some businesses may be to dial back on the products and services they provide, an approach that some leading retailers are already considering.

○ Editing Choices to Boost Well-Being

Whether the issue is horsemeat turning up in beef burgers or doughnuts contributing to obesity, supermarket chains and other retail businesses are under growing pressure to use their influence as market gatekeepers to promote health and well-being through what is sometimes called "choice editing"—for example, by removing from their shelves various items that might be potentially damaging either to people or to the environment.

Supermarkets, some of which have been at the forefront of the movement, have tried such approaches as shifting to compact fluorescent or LED lighting products (and removing incandescent bulbs from the shelves, whether or not customers might still want them) and augmenting their "healthier eating" categories. In other cases, they have invested in improved labeling and consumer information (covering everything from salt content to the conditions in which the hens that laid your eggs were kept), partly to avoid regulation and the wholesale removal of particular products from their shelves.

Most retailers see choice editing as a strategy for improving well-being by offering smarter, more sustainable choices. As noted, the increasing incidence of obesity in developed countries, which is closely linked to the spread of chronic diseases, is a significant challenge. Breakthrough leaders aim to assess how their products and services help fuel the obesity epidemic, which threatens to result in stratospheric health care costs. Some of these, inevitably, will cascade back both to manufacturers and to retailers through such mechanisms as class action suits. Other concerns include reducing or removing those products that are environmentally problematic, that are created using unsustainable components, that depend on child labor, or that rely on poverty-level wages.

Of course, not everyone is thrilled with retailer-driven choice editing. Some people have expressed outrage at the loss of their beloved incandescent lightbulbs, for example. Indeed, traditional-ist consumer activists go so far as to argue that consumers have the right to buy whatever they want, regardless of potentially haz-ardous effects on people or the planet. At the same time, what is important to one consumer may well be of no interest — or in some cases actively offensive — to others. Whether a product is green or organic or locally made might not matter too much to a consumer on a limited budget, for example. As a result, expect the challenge facing retailers to become more intense and complex.

Breakthrough leaders understand that most of today's con-sumers want to purchase and use healthier, greener products, as long as their price and quality expectations are met. The B Team encourages all businesses to look at themselves, their supply chains, and their value webs to create lower-impact, sustainable, locally sourced products. One critical consideration in choice editing, however, is whether consumers are willing to trade performance or price in favor of lower-impact products. It is crucial that we do not leave choice editing entirely in the hands of retail businesses. Governments will continue to have a critically important role to play.

Choice editing has been around for generations, but in the past was mainly practiced by governments. The regulation and eventual removal, for instance, of DDT insecticides from agriculture stemmed from an acknowledgment of the compound's declining benefits, damaging toxicity, and negative environmental effects. In such cases, as with the later removal of PCBs and CFCs, a well-managed market process can ensure that consumers are not too badly inconvenienced. However, some of the challenges we now face—for example, the continuing rise of greenhouse gases in the atmosphere—threaten transitions that could be much more wrenching if governments and business fail to get ahead of the curve.

Producing greener products and services that rely on sustainable components throughout the supply chain often costs more—at least until economies of scale start to kick in—but for smart companies and brands, those costs can be balanced by enhanced reputation and improved customer loyalty.

Choice editing requires breakthrough leaders to think more carefully about what they put into their products and what they leave out. It requires them to think about each and every component that goes into the process—from raw materials and labor to transportation and waste. Increasingly, too, business leaders must consider how their products and other offerings play into concepts like the sharing economy or, more fundamentally still, the circular economy (see Chapter Seven).

o Improving Infrastructures

If we are to continue boosting the well-being of the billions of people currently trapped in poverty or ill health, in addition to those whose wider interests are poorly served, we must invest mightily in infrastructures of all sorts—water, sanitation, electricity, and transport, among others. This means that leaders in all sectors and all geographies must think about smart infrastructures, smart grids, and, ultimately, smarter cities and economies.

Infrastructures are central to the Plan B agenda and to our collective prospects for a sustainable future. That's not to say that the provision of infrastructure is a panacea to the world's ills. Indeed, such infrastructures themselves sometimes have caused considerable second-order problems. For example, London's nineteenth-century sewage system simply dumped sewage into the Thames, where, in 1865, a foundering pleasure steamer's passengers were thought as likely to have died from poisoning as by drowning.

More recently, the power infrastructures that provide electricity create various forms of pollution, including acid rain. The water supply infrastructures of places like Los Angeles have stripped other regions of water, resulting in a drastic depletion of the once-mighty Colorado River and, in the process, forcing communities and states to rethink their own water supplies.[16] By no means finally, today's smart grids could prove to be tomorrow's hacker's paradise.

Our challenge, then, is not simply to invest in and build new infrastructures — including smart grids in the developed world and just about everything in the booming, sprawling cities of the developing world — but to do so in ways that do not create the next generation of problems. That said, improving infrastructure is a necessary component of most attempts to improve the well-being of people and the planet.

Urban planning will play a key role. Some experts note that "by understanding the underlying structure of urban spaces and the importance of social interactions, urban planners, public health officials, and community members may capitalize on opportunities to leverage resources to improve the health and well-being of urban populations and promote social justice and health equity."[17] This is something that the best architects and city planners have long known, even if their insights and principles haven't always made it into the real world.

Although opponents may claim that the costs of building new infrastructure systems and improving existing ones are often prohibitive, the fact is that over time, and as long as issues like corruption are well managed, the benefits generally outweigh the costs. Not only can smart, sustainable infrastructure go far in improving the health and well-being of people and the planet—therefore improving the economic status of billions of people the world over—but some experts estimate there to be a $50 trillion global market in this area over the next decade or so. Even in a world increasingly desensitized to large numbers, that's an extraordinary figure.

Denying or ignoring the importance of infrastructures—be they physical, financial, social, or institutional—can damage health and well-being. In a recent report issued by the U.K.-based Future Communities and the Young Foundation, researchers found that local networks, community experiences, and social infrastructures help build a sense of belonging, identity, and community. The report notes that "'a spiral of decline' can occur when there are problems with the quality of the physical environment, poor local services, and weak social networks in the community.... A number of related social problems are associated with new communities that lack good social infrastructure, including isolation, mental health problems, fear of crime, and issues with community cohesion."[18]

As cities opt for smarter buildings and infrastructures, leaders in every sector must keep a wary eye out for possible unintended consequences. Lorie Wigle, a vice president in McAfee's security fabric program, works every day with the cyber-security challenge. "We see smart grids both as the future and as critical infrastructure that needs to be protected against cyber attack," she says. "According to the U.S. Department of Homeland Security's Cyber Response team, 41 percent of the attacks they responded to in 2012 were in the energy sector. The reality of this threat is also now reflected in utility priorities, and government guidance to them, around the world."

Wigle notes that modernizing grids has wide ramifications. "The actions we're taking to modernize the grid make it more resilient against natural phenomena like weather events and solar storms," she says. "Problems can be detected and corrected more quickly and automatically. This resiliency also applies to cyber attacks. Over time, we must make all our operating systems more secure and more resilient. Weaving the various elements together will allow us to create a 'security fabric' for protecting critical infrastructure. The smart grid is a good place to start, but the same approach also applies to smart cities."

It is increasingly clear that our future well-being will depend on the intelligent design, development, and maintenance of a widening range of infrastructures, both "hard" (like those made out of concrete and steel) and "soft" (those provided through software, education, skills, and institutions). Breakthrough innovation will require constant vigilance as unintended consequences flow through the system and as disruptive innovators trigger resistance from the incumbents whose current business models and other interests are threatened. One way that the disruption can be made more appealing to the public and to decision makers is to frame it in terms of health and well-being.

o Creating New Societal Dreams

Perhaps the most powerful factor shaping our sense of well-being is the prevailing societal dream. Simply stated, the American Dream has been wonderful for its main beneficiaries, but for others it has turned into something of a nightmare.

The term "American Dream," coined only relatively recently — in the 1930s — by historian James Truslow Adams, originally was meant as "that dream of a land in which life should be better and richer and fuller for everyone, with opportunity for each according to ability or achievement.... It is not a dream of motor cars and high wages merely, but a dream of social order in which each man and each woman shall be able to attain to the fullest stature of which they are innately capable, and be recognized by others for what they are, regardless of the fortuitous circumstances of birth or position."[19] In many ways, although perhaps not explicitly here, Adams was talking about happiness, health, and well-being—key tenets of Plan B.

Over time, however, the concept of the American Dream has morphed, and many would conclude that today's American Dream is a radical dilution of Adams's original vision. In fact, because of an endemic failure to track and value the true costs and returns of development, some would now link it with everything from traffic accidents, mental illness, obesity, crime, and rampant materialism to indigenous populations suffering badly from the colonization of their lands. In response, efforts to conjure up a New American Dream have been on the rise.

Organizations like the Center for a New American Dream argue the need to reduce consumption, improve quality of life, protect the environment, and promote social justice—also key goals of Plan B. The Center works with business leaders, communities, and institutions to "conserve natural resources, counter the commercialization of our culture, support community engagement, and promote positive changes in the way goods are produced and consumed. New Dream seeks to change social norms around consumption and consumerism and to support the local movement of individuals and communities pursuing lifestyle and community action."[20]

Although such organizations are trying to shift toward a healthier version of the American Dream, the American Dream itself seems to be losing luster around the world. Today, as a result, some emerging economies want their own dream. Partly this is because they simply don't want to exist in the shadow of America, but it is also partly because they recognize that if the rest of the world were to follow the resource-intensive American Dream, we may all well be doomed.

Peggy Liu of JUCCCE (Joint US-China Cooperation on Clean Energy), a nonprofit organization dedicated to accelerating the greening of China, is one of a number of breakthrough leaders working toward the creation of a more sustainable "China Dream." JUCCCE is looking at the very language used to define and describe this new dream. "The new China Dream is redefining the language of sustainability as a language of prosperity," Liu explains. "It must go beyond, and even exclude, 'sustainable eco-geek' vocabulary, if it is to speak to people in a compelling way. The China Dream is more than a sustainable lifestyle—it is creating a national identity to overlay a five-thousand-year-old culture on top of modern realities. It is giving voice to the new breed of 'China Dreamers,' the newly minted eight hundred million members of the country's middle class."

Whether countries like China and America are willing to reframe and reboot their national dreams remains to be seen, but the good news is that breakthrough-oriented leaders at JUCCCE and elsewhere are thinking in new ways that promise to go far in improving health and embracing well-being.

Social entrepreneurs and intrapreneurs can be key leaders in this area. For them and for other breakthrough leaders, ultimate success will require working with a range of businesses, governments, institutions, organizations, and retailers to incentivize healthier workplaces and lifestyles, edit choices, improve infrastructures, and reframe new dreams of what a happy, healthy society looks like. Another key to improved well-being will be to find ways to level the market playing field for those who are developing and offering solutions to elements of the Breakthrough Challenge, which is the topic of our next chapter.

6

Level the Playing Field

Today's markets are often so skewed toward unsustainable outcomes, toward ultimate breakdown, that to put things right we will need to disrupt today's playing fields, upsetting many incumbents — and tilting the pitch in favor of insurgents determined to tackle the Breakthrough Challenge.

Breakthrough leaders know that it is critically important for the market playing field to be made as level as possible through introducing fairer regulations, rethinking incentives, campaigning against perverse subsidies, and fighting corruption. In contrast, leaders who succumb to short-term thinking, ignoring the future in favor of the next quarter, all too often fail to make the connection between sustainability and a level playing field.

As with other aspects of the Plan B agenda, leveling the playing field will be an immense and ongoing leadership challenge. Meanwhile, with so many competing interests fighting for position, it is understandable that it can be a real stretch for even the most determined contenders to fight for fairness and equality. The task is in a very real sense political, with many business leaders shying away from being involved in progressive policy setting, at least directly. Breakthrough leaders know that they significantly increase their chances of achieving a more level playing field when they

- Speak out in public about the relevant problems, even when their competitors or business federations are energetically opposed to their doing so
- Encourage policymakers and regulators to recognize and address the problem in ways that are well considered, easy to police, and likely to produce the desired outcomes
- Join, support, or form initiatives designed to advance the case for change

CEO David Levine of the American Sustainable Business Council (ASBC) is one of the leaders advancing the case for a level playing field. Founded in 2009, the ASBC's members represent more than 200,000 businesses and 325,000 entrepreneurs, owners, executives, investors, and business professionals. Levine and his team are doing their best to tilt market playing fields toward better outcomes. He notes, "A sustainable market should be structured and managed to be fair, transparent, well regulated, and fully accountable to all participants. Additionally, we must ensure that our democracy — in particular our electoral and legislative process — is not controlled by just the wealthiest, but that we encourage and protect the participation of all."

○ Abiding by the Rules

In essence, the concept of a level playing field equates to fairness. Although history is full of cases in which unfair outcomes have prevailed, our species appears to be hardwired to sense what is fair. Personal interest may well override this sensibility, particularly when the wider system is built on the backs of slaves or on the burning of fossil fuels, for example, but the historical record suggests that such abusive systems are intrinsically vulnerable to disruptive change.

In calling for a leveling of the playing field, generally upward to embrace new standards of fair play, The B Team leaders stress that they are not calling for an everyone-is-equal utopia. Instead, they are pushing toward a future in which every player has an equal chance of success and plays by the same set of rules.

A market playing field can be said to be level if the rules — and their application — do not impede the ability of any player to play fairly and, as a result, potentially successfully. In the very nature of things, it is inevitable that different players in any game — be it poker or the market for oranges or derivatives — will bring to bear different skills, experiences, and combinations of luck and ill fortune to their respective fields of play. The key here is that those playing fields must at least start out on level ground — and there must be mechanisms to ensure that those conditions are maintained over time, by creating clear rules, dispute resolution processes, and enforcement mechanisms.

Despite the self-interested arguments of many lobbyists, government regulations often help to provide (and in some cases impose) fairness, as the essence of the changes they impose is (or should be) that all participants abide by the same rules. For example, architects are meant to abide by the same building codes, material specifications, zoning restrictions, and energy efficiency standards. Similarly, auto designers work with rules specifying such elements as safety features, the placing and brightness of headlamps, and the sort of engine capacities and emission levels that attract various forms of road tax.

Businesspeople rarely call for more rules, but the ASBC's Levine does — and so do The Plan B leaders. "Any market is nothing more and nothing less than a set of rules and conventions negotiated by people through a political process," notes Levine. Good rules help businesses, governments, and NGOs tap into the power of innovation. Rules are essential to a sound economy, and they make it possible for everyone to have a fair crack at the relevant market opportunities.

"Regulations limit the power of old-economy, harmful companies and technologies, and by doing so they promote fair competition, innovation, and change," Levine continues. "They help ensure the stability of the financial system and the adequate flow of capital to develop new opportunities. They protect against the externalization of costs that hurt the environment and the public and ultimately damage the economy itself. Good rules also acknowledge that small and medium-size businesses might need support systems and different iterations of the rules in order to meet the requirements."

The B Team acknowledges that inherited wealth and privilege, the differential power of national economies, the outsize returns that can sometimes come as part of first-mover advantage, and other factors mean that few market playing fields start out level. Even where they do, they can become skewed over time. In some cases, this is simply because some people are better at playing the game, and over time accumulate power and resources as a result. In other cases, some players — and some referees — become involved in progressively more determined efforts to distort the rules, typically through various forms of bribery and corruption.

We see this happen across all walks of life, from sports to politics to business. Most of the time, as already noted, most of us have a pretty acute sense of what is fair and what is not. Indeed, if a significant number of people believe that the system is unfair, weighted against some players and tilted toward others, the chances are that they are right.

It is all too easy, however, for complacent or weak-willed leaders to look the other away, to turn a blind eye. Such failures may stem from legitimate concerns, or they may be the result of more nefarious intentions. The truth is that countries or markets in which there is widespread bribery and corruption, poor market transparency, or limited forms of democratic process and governance are likely to see drastic market distortions favoring those with power and influence.

Of course, this happens everywhere, to some degree. The battle against corruption is never done. Even in democratic countries, the rules of the political game may provide unfair advantage to players with access to money or politicians (or both). The controversies about campaign finance reform in the United States provide just one ongoing example of the inequities that money and power can cause.

By financing political candidates, business players can ensure that rules favoring their own company or industry are drafted and introduced into law. Where rules they don't like already exist, favored treatment may be available, as when U.S. regulators in the Gulf of Mexico failed to control aspects of the oil industry effectively, a dynamic that helped tip the balance in favor of disaster, namely BP's catastrophic Deepwater Horizon oil spill in 2010.

Breakthrough leaders recognize the need for fairness, openness, and transparency to ensure market health, but once such conditions are in place, they also do their utmost to ensure that the odds are stacked—fairly—in their favor. So, for example, much successful innovation ultimately skews the playing field toward the innovators, at least until the new ways of operating become endemic. The state of the market playing field can help or hinder us in the fight for a more sustainable future, so it is critical that this issue be formally on tomorrow's agenda for the global C-suite.

Ensuring that markets are level, fair, and transparent and that all key actors are accountable will require herculean efforts, sustained over time. Among the tools at our disposal are incentives, both financial and nonfinancial—so long as they're used effectively, transparently, and for good.

○ Leveraging the Power of Positive Incentives

In many areas, the challenge today is not so much to preserve the conditions prevailing across an existing playing field but to tilt the playing field and even create new ones. This is where well-designed incentives can play a role — across markets, through supply chains, and in the heart of leading companies and other business organizations.

As Peter Bakker, president of the World Business Council for Sustainable Development (WBCSD), points out, "Incentives are crucial, both inside and outside companies. When I left TNT, 50 percent of the bonus was being paid on nonfinancial data. Until the rules of the game have changed, every incentive package of top management should include a significant percentage of sustainability-related targets that are linked to the wider science-based targets that inform us on things like planetary boundaries. Once the rules have changed, we can move away from that approach, because everything will be captured in the share price. But that is quite some years away, I'm afraid."

The question is whether we can afford to be so slow. Breakthrough leaders understand that rewards for positive behavior can go a lot farther than punishments for bad behavior. Positive incentives can do much to encourage organizations across all sectors to work toward better outcomes. "Views vary on what is a good incentive and which not," notes Unilever CEO Paul Polman, but "it is far more effective to encourage positive behavior. I think The B-Team has a responsibility to help government encourage positive behavior. For example, in the U.K., people were offered a tax benefit for the installation of solar panels."

Sometimes the use of positive incentives requires some creative thinking — or at least a twist on the traditional approach. For example, Polman notes that one of the more contentious external issues Unilever has faced — the use of palm oil — has forced him and the relevant parts of the business to think of positive incentives in new ways. "The hard reality," he says, "is that it is still cheaper for companies to buy nonsustainable goods such as palm oil, something we pay $25 million for. However, we are now helping to publish the names of the companies that are buying sustainable palm oil — and, de facto, showing the companies that are not buying it. Now we can use this market information as leverage and go to the banks and promote policies that stop them lending to companies that participate in deforestation."

That said, even progressive leaders like Polman and other B Team members rely on the rest of the world eventually catching up — and that often depends on the existence and enforcement of rules that help to level the playing field for all players. Breakthrough leaders can promote and lobby for change in the ways governments incentivize the creation and use of more environmentally sustainable products and materials. If, for example, import taxes or even VAT were linked to an index of environmental or social performance, a more sustainable product or material could end up costing less than rival products that have yet to internalize the relevant externalities. This would make for a much quicker shift toward more sustainable market offerings.

Business leaders can — indeed must — lobby for such progressive change, despite the challenges they will encounter in the process. One of today's most vexing problems is that the largest environmental and social impacts are usually happening a long way away in a given supply chain, often in countries where the political and cultural conditions are very different, weakening the effect of incentives that would work well elsewhere. Over time, too, incentives can become so entrenched that, although once positive, they are perverted to the point that they are no longer beneficial or are actively pernicious.

○ Removing Perverse Subsidies

Incentives are endemic in all markets, whatever champions of free markets may claim or want, and often date back to earlier eras and reflect previous priorities. Over time, entire industries can become dependent on various external forms of support, such as tax incentives and subsidies. Governments also often seek to protect national champions, strategic industries, or high-profile (or politically influential) companies that either are threatened by innovations developed elsewhere or are struggling to develop their own innovations in the teeth of foreign competition. This can be seen in any number of industries, including the coal, fisheries, aerospace, and defense sectors.

A central problem is that many of the incentives in the current system conspire to maintain the old order, regardless of the effects in terms of negative externalities. Governments often make things worse, without intending to do so, offering what are called "perverse subsidies" to industries driven by illusions of continuing (even infinite) growth. Examples include those that hoover their way through overexploited fisheries or those still pursuing new coal, tar sand, or deep ocean oil, despite the fact that—in a sane and sustainable future—they may never be able to burn the resulting fuels.

No single government is the lone culprit when it comes to perverse incentives. The logic of international competition means that such subsidies abound across countries and sectors. As professor Norman Myers noted some years back in *The Encyclopedia of Earth*, "In Germany, for instance, subsidies for coal mining are so large that it would be economically efficient for the government to close down all the mines and send the workers home on full pay for the rest of their lives. The environment would benefit too: less coal pollution such as acid rain and global warming."[1]

Evidence of market distortions is everywhere. In the United States, for example, a gallon of bottled water costs as much as three times more than a gallon of gas, thanks in large part to subsidies to the gas industry.[2] In the United Kingdom, where farming subsidies total more than £3 billion, a recent study found that the public is being shortchanged "by billions of pounds a year in lost environmental and social benefits."[3]

The B Team leaders conclude that perverse subsidies distort economies and wreak havoc on people and the planet, putting our common future at risk. Perverse incentives can spur the exploitation of climate-destabilizing fossil fuels; keep at sea (and even promote the further expansion of) fishing fleets that threaten to collapse an increasing number of fisheries; and accelerate the effective "quarrying" of potentially renewable resources like timber and water. At the same time, perverse subsidies also can discourage the development and scaling of more sustainable technologies and business models.

Happily, perverse subsidies are coming under intensifying pressure, although often for rather different reasons. According to Fatih Birol, who heads the International Energy Agency (IEA), it is the growing cost of subsidies, rather than worries about climate change, that is making them increasingly vulnerable. In the fossil fuels area, governments found their budgets under pressure as global oil prices doubled between 2009 and 2012.[4] The cost of government subsidies for fossil fuels rose from $311 billion in 2009 to $544 billion in 2012, according to IEA estimates. Once lost taxes are factored in, this figure rises to around $2 trillion, equal to around 8 percent of government revenues.

Worse, some of these subsidies are perverse in multiple dimensions. Research by the International Monetary Fund suggests that only 7 percent of fuel subsidies in poor countries reach the bottom 20 percent of households, with 43 percent ending up with the richest 20 percent.[5]

Even where perverse incentives do not apply, there is often a need for government action to raise the rewards for both responsible operations and breakthrough innovation. As Mark Goyder, founder director of Tomorrow's Company, a London-based global think tank, notes, "Governments and regulators (and ultimately, institutional investors) need to find ways of rewarding the good stewards and offering fewer privileges to the predatory. In the end, we need clear and shared criteria that can assess businesses by their stewardship, not their ownership." The aim will be to favor "businesses that are clear about their purpose and their mandate, that have a capacity to renew and improve themselves, that sense and help shape the landscape around them, and that consciously balance the short term with the long term."

There is evidence that at least some governments are waking up to the ill effects of perverse subsidies. In October 2013, for example, European Union lawmakers voted against subsidies to build new fishing vessels, a move that may help bring an end to decades of overfishing in Europe and, eventually, elsewhere in the world's oceans.

Of course, governments don't act alone when it comes to doling out perverse subsidies. Businesses, lobbyists, and politicians often work hand in hand to craft legislation, tax breaks, and other rules that benefit particular industries and sectors. Although it is understood that organizations must do what they can to ensure success, The B Team leaders also insist that these efforts cannot be at the cost of people and the planet.

On the flipside, the challenge of incentivizing companies to develop and deploy environment- and people-friendly products, materials, and services will rise up the policy agenda.

Positive incentives could be introduced, for example, in the form of a reduction in corporate taxes for those organizations that meet sustainability standards, which could go a long way toward accelerating the mainstreaming of the relevant practices.

o Joining Forces

Where elements of the existing system handicap efforts to move toward more sustainable outcomes, leaders must call them out and work together to remove at least the worst barriers to progressive change. We need balanced and open debate about major new rules, to ensure that they are well designed and likely to be effective and fair when in force.

Paul Polman has been trying to do just that, aiming to tilt the playing field within the company, across its supply chain, and, ultimately, in the wider world. As CEO of one of the world's largest multinational consumer goods companies, he has been striving to shift the paradigm that has too many leaders working under the mistaken belief that sustainability and profits are mutually exclusive. He has been guiding Unilever and its wider business ecosystem toward the goal of improving "the hygiene habits of more than a billion people by 2020 by encouraging hand washing and providing safe, affordable drinking water in developing countries. Those goals are part of a sustainability strategy [that Polman] says can double Unilever's sales while halving its environmental footprint."[6]

Unilever's Sustainable Living Plan is a particularly bold undertaking. With three overarching goals[7] and seven related commitments, the plan affects tens of thousands of employees and millions of consumers. It is designed to reach right across Unilever's worldwide offices and out through its global supply chains and value webs. This is a powerful example of the key point that leveling playing fields, more often than not, must involve leveling not downward, but upward.

Such actions are not much use if just one company moves, however. Breakthrough leaders know that they need others to swing in and compete on the basis of the new rules. This is an unusual circumstance: they want to see competitors move in sooner rather than later.

Indeed, alongside level playing fields and good refereeing, competition is the key to making markets work. At their best, business leaders face the competition head-on, as when Ford developed the EcoBoost engine in response to market pressure from hybrid vehicle producers like Toyota. Although Toyota has long been the leader in hybrids, Ford has not been standing still. Its one-liter (nonhybrid) EcoBoost engine has garnered a number of awards, including International Engine of the Year in both 2012 and 2013. Remarkably, it gets more than sixty-five miles per gallon of gasoline with CO_2 emissions of just 99g/km, a truly breakthrough achievement — although not yet the universal answer to tomorrow's sustainable access and mobility needs.

Avoiding destructive practices doesn't just mean making better products or improving materials along supply chains. In some cases, business must lobby politicians and other leaders alike in order to ensure that new rules are well considered, intelligently designed, and fairly and effectively implemented. In other cases, it may prove to be strategically sensible to slow the running down of old industries to ensure that they operate as cash cows, providing the financial springboards needed to launch into new technologies or business models.

Such complex games mean that the players must work out how to join forces in new and above-board ways. One way leaders can do this is to join and support organizations that are on the leading edge of business-led change platforms, including the WBCSD and The B Team. The key will be to combine forces and lobby for the new market conditions needed to get new products and services, new technologies, and new industries off the ground.

○ Avoiding Corruption

The lobbying of politicians and governments by business isn't automatically a bad thing, whatever activists may think. Breakthrough leaders can bring much hard-won expertise to the process of drafting and implementing new rules. In some cases, business actively takes the lead, proposing new rules that can help push the needle toward the necessary changes, though we must be careful to ensure that such actions do not lead to undue influence and, ultimately, involve full-blown bribery and other forms of corruption.

Generally speaking, corruption is defined as the abuse of entrusted power for private gain. According to the world's leading anticorruption NGO, Transparency International (TI), it can be classified as grand, petty, and political, depending on the amounts of money lost and the sector where it occurs.[8] Significantly, TI was founded by government and business leaders determined to tackle the issue head-on. Having seen corruption's impact during his work in East Africa, retired World Bank official Peter Eigen, together with nine allies, set up what was originally a tiny organization in Berlin.

At the time, corruption was largely a taboo topic. As the TI website notes, "Many companies regularly wrote off bribes as business expenses in their tax filings, the graft of some longstanding heads of state was legendary, and many international agencies were resigned to the fact that corruption would sap funding from many development projects around the world. There was no global convention aimed at curbing corruption, and no way to measure [it] at the global scale."[9]

Of course, a solid foundation in ethics won't solve every problem, and the lobbying world isn't the sole bastion of corrupt practices. These kinds of destructive practices exist everywhere. The fight against them has to be vigilant, courageous, and constant. A growing number of business leaders are working to root it out where they find it, but they underscore the scale of the problem they face. Polman notes, "We are pushing for transparency and anticorruption standards in markets in which corruption has hundreds of years of history, such as India and regions like Africa."

Excused in many ways as "part of the culture" or "the way things have always been done around here," bribery and corruption make decision making more personal, more tribal, and more corrosive of long-term thinking. The result, over time, can be market distortions on a truly epic scale, leading to playing fields that are tilted at extreme angles, making fair play impossible and ensuring that the returns are anything but true. Things can change, however. In China, for example, we have seen the extraordinary spectacle of 5-star hotels trying to drop a star and return to 4-star status, as the government cracks down on corrupt officials who stay in top-flight hotels,[10] yet China still routinely tries corruption activists in secret.[11]

To curb corruption and ensure that the markets they operate in are progressively cleaned up, businesses leaders must ensure that their organizations and value webs have strong ethical foundations that do not permit unethical behavior in any form, both within the organization and across its supply chains and other relationships. In addition, clear policies and penalties must be embedded in all processes and organizational structures. Auditing and controlling measures and procedures as well as whistleblower hotlines must be in place and regularly monitored by the board and C-suite.

○ Evolving the Playing Field

One challenge we can expect to face in the coming decades will be the need to regulate problematic, unsustainable activities — and then to police those regulations effectively around the world. It is not yet clear how this can best be done, with new rules and regulations in one area creating unintended market distortions in others. For this reason, The B Team views better governance as a central challenge.[12]

No international organization today — be it the United Nations, the OECD, Interpol, or NATO — has the ability to do this properly. This suggests either that such institutions need to be profoundly changed or that we will be forced to evolve new ones that are fit for this purpose. This likely will be another case of "both-and." Normally, such change comes only during or after major wars or economic discontinuities like protracted depressions, but the idea behind Plan B is that leaders of every sort now have a vested interest in helping jump-start the process.

With so many other things on their plate, even some high-profile leaders may question how to proceed on the regulatory front — or even whether it is, in fact, up to them to find ways to level all the playing fields in which their businesses operate. Behind closed doors, some will question whether it's really up to them to fight against bribery and corruption or change the way lobbying is done, for example.

At a time when their businesses face uncertain economic prospects, with consumers demanding more for less, and shareholders and financial analysts pushing for those extra pennies in earnings every quarter, business leaders may find it all too easy to push aside what seem to be intangible, more distant issues. They do so at the peril of betraying the long-term interests of their organizations, let alone living up to tomorrow's moral standards. That's why we must refresh the old market rules and impose new ones. Only by doing so can we ensure outcomes that are fair both to those alive today and to future generations.

That is why we so admire the work of organizations like Transparency International. The movement, now present in more than a hundred countries, strives for "a world in which government, business, civil society and the daily lives of people are free of corruption" through such actions as holding anticorruption conventions, prosecuting corrupt leaders, seizing illicitly gained riches, supporting fair and free national elections, and holding companies accountable for their behavior.[13] All these are necessary conditions if we are to succeed in leveling tomorrow's market playing field; so too is much greater market transparency generally, the challenge we turn to in the next chapter.

7

Pursue Full Transparency

Open, accountable forms of transparency anchor all other priorities and objectives of The B Team; they are a sine qua non. Useful transparency involves sharing the right information at the right time with the right users or stakeholders—and in the right ways.

The public appetite and demand for transparency—both in the public and private sectors—has been growing for decades, having been the focus of any number of NGO campaigns and of right-to-know legislation in some countries. In the United States, for example, the Enron debacle of the early 2000s sent transparency considerations rocketing up the political agenda. In the wake of this scandal and others in a similar vein, legislation like the Sarbanes-Oxley Act of 2002 (SOX) aimed to impose new market standards. These increasingly require corporate officials to sign off on key financial information in the hope that by forcing business leaders to take personal responsibility, market stakeholders could be reassured that the information they receive is accurate, thorough, and current.

That at least has been the theory. Whether SOX has indeed helped improve financial transparency as once hoped is debatable. What is beyond dispute is the notion that the world requires much more than a few additional signatures on some financial paperwork in order to create the market conditions necessary for the transition to a truly sustainable future.

That's why The B Team leaders have worked to ensure that their Plan B prioritizes full transparency — transparency that goes way beyond financial reporting to illuminate all aspects of an organization and its supply chain. Much of this new transparency will require improved reporting and true cost accounting (as discussed in Chapter Three), although new forms of technology will also prove critical. Human nature being what it is, though, we can expect the equivalent of an arms race as transparency-inducing technologies are countered by new encryption methods and other stealth-promoting measures specifically designed to keep certain actions and activities out of the public eye.

New tools and platforms are constantly emerging that offer enhanced levels of information to business customers, consumers, and investors on what particular sectors and companies are doing. Firms like Paris-based EcoVadis, for example, provide business-to-business players with increasing access to supply chain data and supplier profiles.[1] Consumers can use new tools like GoodGuide, a service that enables shoppers in supermarkets to scan the bar codes of products on the shelves (or, potentially, on online platforms like Amazon) to get an instant download on the performance of products, brands, and companies in relation to the shopper's priority issues (for example, obesity, animal welfare, or climate change). For investors, there is a growing array of analysis and intelligence services, one of the most notable being the triple-bottom-line-oriented Dow Jones Sustainability Indexes. Emerging tools like ecological and social footprinting, the EP&L and SP&L approaches, and various forms of social ROI accounting can help us uncover new trends, relationships, and other market intelligence.

Over time, given the way that markets evolve, such pioneers know that they risk seeing key elements of their breakthrough offerings absorbed into the mainstream. This might happen, for example, when supermarkets start to offer some elements of a GoodGuide-like service, whether licensed from the inventors or developed in parallel form, or when an agency like Bloomberg starts to stream the sort of information that once was available only from specialist providers like the Dow Jones Sustainability Indexes team.

Corporate reporting is but one part of the shift toward a more transparent economy, though it can be seen as a useful starting point. One key trend, as already explained, is the move toward integrated reporting, driven by players like the Global Reporting Initiative and the International Integrated Reporting Council. Before we look forward, however, let's take a quick look back at what brought us to this point in the game.

o Doing Business in the Goldfish Bowl

The wider corporate transparency movement has been evolving for many decades. In the late 1970s, for example, one of us (John Elkington) was a cofounder of a business intelligence firm, Environmental Data Services (ENDS). Strikingly, although ENDS had a parent company that was widely respected in the world of industrial relations, it took nearly a year for the ENDS team to gain entry to the first company to investigate how its management perceived and managed issues like safety, health, and environmental protection. Business leaders were gun-shy at the time, convinced that anyone interested in such issues was viscerally antibusiness and anticapitalism.

Nowadays, by contrast, business leaders around the world increasingly take it for granted that the outside world has a right to know (and will likely insist on knowing) much more about their internal decisions and operations—information that not so long ago would have been held much closer to corporate chests. They may not like the trend, but smart business leaders know that these days it isn't so much a question of whether key information gets out into the public domain, but of how—and of who ends up in control of the process.

Later, as cofounder of SustainAbility, John would be a pioneer in the field of corporate environmental reporting. One senior executive from Shell explained to him in 1986 that the oil company would never produce sustainable development reports, "because we are too big and too complex." Ironically, Shell became the first Fortune 500 company to publish a sustainability report, with the title *People, Planet & Profits*. The year: 1997.

That was also the year that the Global Reporting Initiative (GRI) was founded in Boston, to drive triple-bottom-line reporting worldwide. Since then, the corporate reporting trend has run the gamut from environmental reporting (whose mainstreaming you can roughly date from 1990, when two companies—Monsanto in the United States and Norsk Hydro in Norway—produced the first voluntary environmental reports) through to various forms of sustainability reporting, and now we see the accelerating shift toward integrated reporting.

Today we see a new wave, with a growing number of business leaders not simply responding under pressure to make public new forms of data and information. Instead, they are pushing the envelope in such fields as footprinting and accounting. Some also are beginning to call publicly for changes in the market rules covering transparency, accountability, and reporting.

Although there have been many transparency hiccups over the years, no one should doubt how far we have already come in this area. Thousands of companies now produce annual sustainability reports, with a growing number of analysts using at least some of the resulting information to analyze corporate risk profiles and investment prospects. That said, tens of thousands of multinational companies around the world still do not report, among them most family businesses, most small and medium-size enterprises, and most state-owned enterprises.

This is a major challenge for anyone who sees sound information as a key resource not just in running national economies but, over time, in learning how to manage the planet itself—particularly as we continue to press up against planetary boundaries.

Nor is this simply society's or the future's loss. By not reporting on key issues like sustainability and well-being, laggard businesses and industries fail to present investors and other stakeholders with a full accounting of the state of their operations. In some cases, this may mean that their efforts are not properly valued. Elsewhere, the evidence confirms that, time and again, such conditions create complacency, deceit, and market bubbles and crashes.

A key part of tomorrow's challenge will be to make the next generation of transparency, accounting, reporting, and assurance tools increasingly accessible and, critically, easy to use both in business and among stakeholders at large, including investors. Farsighted organizations are already working hard toward this goal.

○ Embracing Integrated Reporting

One of the leading initiatives already mentioned in this area has been the International Integrated Reporting Council (IIRC), "a global coalition of regulators, investors, companies, standard setters, the accounting profession and NGOs."[2] The IIRC champions integrated reporting (often rendered as <IR>), which is "a process founded on integrated thinking that results in a periodic integrated report by an organization about value creation over time and related communications regarding aspects of value creation. An integrated report is a concise communication about how an organization's strategy, governance, performance and prospects, in the context of its external environment, lead to the creation of value in the short, medium and long term."[3]

The B Team and IIRC see eye-to-eye on the integrated reporting imperative, both arguing that this form of corporate reporting should become the norm. IIRC CEO Paul Druckman points out that greater transparency is a global trend with wide and growing support. "In developing economies, especially, businesses, investors, and stock exchanges also see transparency as a powerful driver for attracting inward investment and providing an important competitive advantage," he says. "For example, at the Rio+20 summit, the push for businesses to be more transparent in their disclosures around sustainability information came not from policymakers but from an investor-led coalition with over $2 trillion of capital behind it. With capital markets now recognizing transparency as essential, and leading the charge for change at a global level, it is more likely that initiatives like integrated reporting will move into the mainstream."

It's no accident, then, that Plan B calls for governments, businesses, NGOs, and other organizations to improve reporting on all fronts as a means to address those same system-level challenges. Finding solutions will require breakthrough leaders to think—and act—in new ways. This will include developing and using approaches that go way beyond today's financial reports, regardless of how transparent they might be. The goal for tomorrow's leaders will be to paint a full picture of their operations across the complex landscapes of risk and opportunity thrown up by the ever-shifting forces of globalization and by growing acknowledgment of the need to tackle the Breakthrough Challenge.

In the process, we must hope that more business leaders will wake up to the need to work together to call for improved reporting rules and standards. "Changing the rules on reporting through public policy can have a very powerful effect," says Ernst Ligteringen, CEO of the GRI. "Many governments are now looking for effective policies to promote universal sustainability reporting for defined classes of larger companies. Their initiatives range from 'Report or Explain' [as in why a particular company or organization doesn't report] policies, which would still leave sustainability reporting as a voluntary exercise, through to countries and stock exchanges making sustainability reporting mandatory. Once companies get used to this and experience the benefits of sustainability reporting, political space opens up to raise the bar."

The goal isn't simply to change the frequency, format, and content of company reports. Over time, breakthrough leaders will view corporate disclosure and reporting processes as a means of catalyzing something much more profound. "In the end, GRI's work isn't just about reforming reporting," Ligteringen stresses, "but more fundamentally about changing mind-sets—the mind-sets of directors, managers, and every worker in companies, and mind-sets among investors, customers, and analysts."

The GRI, the IIRC, the Carbon Disclosure Project, and other similar organizations are trying to do just that—and the evidence suggests that their work is beginning to pay off. Ligteringen reports that "over 80 percent of the Fortune 250 and well over half of the S&P 500" are now using the type of sustainability reporting that the GRI espouses. He says, too, that the use of sustainability and integrated reporting has spread well beyond North America, Europe, and Japan to Brazil, China, and India, for example.

This kind of growth is encouraging, although some would argue that it's not spreading nearly far or fast enough, that too often the result is just another long report, that it's read by few people, and that it doesn't affect the heart and soul of business itself, as it is often put together by a specialized department without ever being used in day-to-day business operations.

Integrated reporting, too, is still seen as an in-your-face challenge to many business leaders, particularly those who persist in believing that enhanced financial reporting is more than enough when it comes to transparency. For such people, integrated reporting may seem superfluous or something solely for companies with major brands or reputations to protect. But those who have been through the process of opening the corporate kimono know different.

"Many directors and managers have told us that sustainability was originally a very abstract concept to them, one that they were struggling with until they started to do sustainability reporting and use the GRI Guidelines," recalls Ligteringen. "This, they typically say, made sustainability tangible and real to them—giving them a handle to begin defining their strategy and managing their performance. This works through various phases, from do-less-harm approaches through to zero waste and other more radical approaches to reforming business models."

In simple terms, integrated reporting requires leaders to disclose both their financial and nonfinancial performance. It requires them to examine internal and external drivers for both performance and change, to look at and disclose governance and risk factors and challenges, and to mine related data and quantify their findings. It absolutely does not mean that companies should staple together their financial and nonfinancial reports, however nicely designed the ultimate package may be.

For those who take this route, professionally managed and properly applied integrated reporting can lead to clear and important benefits. Among other things, it can help improve decision making, encourage integrated thinking, enable better business practices, and provide more detailed information to stakeholders.[4] In the wider world, key stakeholders are already making use of both sustainability and integrated reports, mining the data for crucial information about a variety of organizations and industries.

As the GRI's Ligteringen notes, "Current users include a mix of directors and managers within businesses, as well as specialist fund managers and analysts, rating and index providers, specialist media, specific community groups or NGOs, and labor organizations. And, of course, other companies—including competitors. The likes of Bloomberg are now mining these reports and making sustainability data on over four thousand companies available on their terminals. Analysts working with the specialist funds of the largest asset managers say that sustainability reports are their first source of publicly available data."

Of course, investors and other financial stakeholders are still determined to access full and transparent financial reports—these are and will remain crucial sources of information about any business organization. Nevertheless, the leading edge of sustainability reporting and integrated reporting provides additional insight in the quest to provide full transparency, allowing stakeholders to discern interesting new patterns visible across a growing range of issues and (the ultimate goal) to pull multiple dimensions together into a single view and a single dashboard.

o Shrinking Our Footprints

Too often, most of the social and environmental consequences of our actions and consumption patterns can be filed under the heading "out of sight, out of mind." The central purpose of footprinting is to bring these impacts increasingly into view in ways that make it possible to link, relate, and compare impacts created at different levels in the system. These may include industry sectors, urban regions, national economies, and, ultimately, the global economic system.

One of the fastest-developing areas in recent years has been ecological footprinting, and the leading organization here is the Global Footprint Network (GFN). Cofounder Susan Burns sees important progress in the field, noting that the concept is already mainstream in the United States and Europe. The challenge, however, is to move from having people accept the concept to using it to push toward action in the real world. "While there is widespread awareness among decision makers of the fact that we live on a limited planet and that we are in ecological overshoot, major institutions—from development banks to finance ministries—have not made significant changes to their policies, priorities, systems, rewards, and metrics," Burns reports. "When we engage with decision makers, we demonstrate this and provide tools they need to make this real in their institutions."

Although still largely invisible from the perspective of the global C-suite, the evolution of ecological footprinting has been extraordinary. From its origins with Mathis Wackernagel and William Rees, followed by the publication of the book *Our Ecological Footprint*, the method quickly spread around the world, initially via academics and grassroots organizations. Then national footprint numbers were published in WWF's *Living Planet* report, and the concept began to gain mainstream attention. Soon the idea began to be picked up by influential people and news media, from Tony Blair, at the time prime minister of the United Kingdom, to the *Economist*.

It is now clear to many that footprinting, as Burns notes, has "great potential to help move humanity out of what is called 'ecological overshoot,' both because of the uniqueness of the metric but also because of its 'stickiness'—in other words, its strength as an idea or meme." Just as a bank statement tracks income against expenditures, the ecological footprint measures humanity's demand for and supply of natural resources and ecological services.

The data are sobering. The evidence suggests that in approximately eight months, we now demand more renewable resources and CO_2 sequestration than the planet can provide for an entire year. One way that the GFN works to bring these trends to public attention is through what it calls "Earth Overshoot Day"—the approximate date our resource consumption for a given year exceeds the planet's ability to replenish.[5] In 1993, for example, Earth Overshoot Day fell on October 21. By 2013, it fell on September 22, and by 2013, it was August 20.[6] As one measure of impact, Earth Overshoot Day reached over two hundred million people on the Web in 2013 alone.

Given current trends in consumption, the GFN notes, one thing is painfully clear: Earth Overshoot Day arrives earlier each year. Our demand for renewable ecological resources and the services they provide is now equivalent to that of more than 1.5 Earths. The data show that we are now on track to require the resources of two planets well before 2050.

○ Redefining P&L and ROI

So how can we take all of this national footprinting data and create the sort of numbers that will register in boardrooms and C-suites? That's where techniques like the environmental profit and loss (EP&L) and social profit and loss (SP&L) approaches fit in. As already noted, they build off a long history of attempts to account for social and environmental impacts. These include, most importantly, full cost accounting (discussed in Chapter Three), environmental accounting and auditing, social accounting and auditing, and a range of approaches clustered around efforts to calculate the social return on investment.

To make all of this more relevant to accountants and, critically, to business leaders like chief financial officers, one of us (Jochen Zeitz) pioneered the EP&L accounting approach at German sportswear brand Puma and, later, across the brands operated by its Paris-based owner, the holding company Kering. The EP&L was seen as the first step toward a full—and increasingly integrated—set of triple-bottom-line accounts. The numbers reported turned out to be very substantial. When Puma released its first EP&L accounts in 2011, for example, it reported an "impact of €51 million resulting from land use, air pollution and waste along the value chain added to previously [the] announced €94 million for GHG emissions and water consumption."[7] The total environmental loss was pushing toward half the company's reported profit that year.

The EP&L approach aims to address a key criticism of current nonfinancial reporting: that most company reports do not push far enough back through their supply chains to give a true sense of their overall environmental or social footprints. True, we are still a very long way from the point where every organization feels it has no choice but to embrace this tool, but the pace of experimentation is accelerating. Indeed, Kering announced in 2011 that each of its luxury and sport and lifestyle brands would implement a group EP&L by 2016.[8]

The evolutionary process has been helped along by partner organizations like Trucost and PwC. "Companies—big and small—are now reliant on global supply chains, making their environmental footprint much larger than many realize," explains Alan McGill, a partner in PwC's sustainability and climate change practice. "Assigning economic values to the environmental impact of a company's operations enables a business to tackle vital questions, not just about environmental impacts, but about business risk, costs savings and finding new ways to become more effective. Without measuring them, the impacts cannot be managed, or reduced."[9] Clearly, this emerging area of business need represents a major potential opportunity space for such service providers.

At Trucost, the mood is also strikingly upbeat. "It is possible to directly engage finance professionals with these metrics," says Richard Mattison, CEO of Trucost. Even CFOs are now coming on board, he reports. "Since the publication of the Puma EP&L, we have seen a significant increase in interest from finance directors and CFOs seeking to understand how they can use similar metrics."

Trucost calls the EP&L "a proxy for nature's invoice,"[10] a notion that The B Team leaders strongly endorse. The tool allows organizations to assess the cost of their environmental impact, both within their own walls and throughout their supply chains and value webs. By measuring and applying an overarching metric to the costs of such things as land use, water use, and CO_2 output, the EP&L approach allows organizations to paint a true picture of the actual costs of producing their goods and services. This promises to be a key stepping-stone toward the sort of full transparency called for by The B Team.

An SP&L approach to accounting, which we might see as a proxy for society's invoice, also will be crucially important in the pursuit of both corporate and market transparency. When Puma's parent company first tested the feasibility of following on from the EP&L by creating a real-world SP&L, all but one of the stakeholders interviewed thought it was doable. That said, some cautioned that it could take considerable resources and much time to develop the approach fully. Areas that potentially fall within the scope of SP&L reporting include the well-being of employees, the development of human capital, working conditions and other relevant aspects of company operations, product life-cycle issues, and community development.

As with the EP&L, the idea here is that the SP&L approach will allow organizations to measure the development (or erosion) of their human and social capital and, consequently, to develop policies geared toward mitigating related risks. So, for instance, if an organization determines that working conditions are poor, costly, and ineffective, it can apply a cost to those conditions, assess the scale of that cost over time, and create new policies to mitigate the conditions and the associated risks.

Without measuring such factors, companies can find themselves operating in the dark. Currently, they have no real way to manage social costs at a time when stakeholders see them as increasingly important, nor do other stakeholders have any structured way to assess the social capital of a given organization and discuss its valuation and management with leadership.

Obviously, as Puma was warned, measuring social issues can be a tricky, political, and often highly politicized task. But this doesn't mean that it shouldn't be attempted. Organizations like Puma, Kering, and the World Business Council for Sustainable Development have been paving the way, helping kick-start the conversation. Breakthrough leaders who truly wish to pursue full transparency for their companies and industries must find ways not only to keep the conversation going but also to measure, report on, and manage the key social impacts of their operations and plans.

The Social Return on Investment (SROI) community also has been developing ways to measure and value social factors. The central idea is to include the values (rather than simply the value) of people typically excluded from markets in the same terms as used in markets, where money is the main metric. SROI involves seven key principles and related steps: involve stakeholders, understand what changes, value the things that matter, include only what is material, do not overclaim, be transparent, and verify the results.[11] The approach requires leaders to consider a mix of financial, quantitative, and qualitative data, and can require new forms of judgment and analysis.

The ultimate aim is to give people a more powerful voice in resource allocation decisions. In headlines, the SROI approach is geared toward understanding, measuring, and managing "the value of the social, economic and environmental outcomes created by an activity or an organization."[12] Not surprisingly, perhaps, some of the more conservative business leaders insist that SROI is a controversial tool of dubious value. They argue that it is impossible to quantify such intangible aspects of what an organization does. Some even state publicly that it is dangerous to try to assign a value to social capital.[13] However, The B Team leaders conclude that such approaches are generating the necessary experiments that will drive the evolution of a critical new dimension of accounting, reporting, and, ultimately, valuation.

That said, there is an important debate to be had about whether measuring social capital and quantifying it into a single ratio is possible, and, if it is possible, whether it is useful in investment management decisions. The B Team leaders are convinced that it could be helpful — that it would provide a crucial opportunity to mine important information for useful clues that can help paint a fuller picture of the costs and benefits of an organization's activities.

o Harnessing Big Data

As all this information-gathering activity gains speed around the globe, an obvious question arises: What to do with the results? Individual businesses can use the data to help improve the efficiency and wider performance of their operations and supply chains, but something else is needed to make sense of these information flows at the level of the wider system.

The good news is that the rapidly emerging big data trend — despite the understandable controversies regarding privacy and cybersnooping — potentially provides a powerful means to track the systemwide impacts of our environmental and social footprints, as well as of our consumer choices and activities.

As we are forced to take increasing control over the interactions between our economies, societies, and the wider biosphere, such technologies can only become more important.

Mining data in the right way allows business organizations both to avoid key risks and to unlock new forms of value through their operations and supply chains. By examining and measuring the financial, environmental, and social aspects of their organizations, leaders are better able to manage risk, cut costs, and craft policies, strategies, and business models that align more powerfully with the Breakthrough Challenge agenda.

The key, of course, is to pull together and analyze the right data. More data alone aren't necessarily a better thing—in fact, floods of superfluous data can easily obscure important issues and lead managers astray. Breakthrough leaders know they must work together to find ways not only to successfully gather and mine all the relevant data but also to break it down into manageable, useful chunks that help drive and steer progress in the real world.

A growing number of businesses are working hard to do just that. Consider BT PLC, a U.K.-based provider of telecommunications networks that has customers in more than 170 countries. The company provides fixed-line services, broadband, mobile, and television products and services as well as networked IT services to consumers, small- and medium-size enterprises, and the public sector.[14] Between 2011 and 2013, BT mined and analyzed data to examine the entire carbon footprint of its business, discovering that emissions outside its own direct control accounted for 92 percent of the total; 64 percent of that impact was just in BT's upstream supply chain. When that supply chain involves seventeen thousand suppliers around the world and products and services worth £9.7 billion, this inevitably leads to data complexity. However, with this information in hand, BT was able to highlight carbon hotspot areas, revealing business opportunities for reducing costs and carbon.[15]

Ford, probably still America's best-known automaker, also sees mining big data as a key part of its sustainability efforts. According to John Viera, the company's global director of sustainability, for more than a decade the automaker has been using "analytics and big data to minimize Ford's environmental impact and improve its bottom line."[16] The resulting market and scientific intelligence has enabled the company to create ecofriendly products that not only cost less to produce but also help consumers save money on gas and maintenance—potentially a triple dividend in terms of people, planet, and profit.

"Analytics permeates almost every aspect of sustainability at Ford," as the company puts it, "helping to chart paths to a cleaner, brighter, better world and a stronger business. The amount of available data is growing fast: Ford researchers have begun experimenting with vehicles that produce 250 gigabytes of data an hour. More information leads to further improvements in increasing fuel economy and reducing vehicle emissions." In a nutshell, "Ford considers big data and analytics the next frontier for innovation, competition and productivity, with new opportunities emerging such as green routing, that allows consumers to optimize driving routes to minimize their impact on local air quality."[17]

Similarly, delivery giant UPS is mining big data to save millions of dollars on gas every year. By capturing and analyzing key data points, UPS has been able to optimize delivery routes such that the company saves millions of gallons of gas, and drivers are able to shave meaningful time off their routes, improving efficiency on several levels.[18]

The benefits of big data are increasingly obvious in the global C-suite, although inevitably many businesses will struggle to develop and apply the necessary technology and skills. The field is still emergent, but it is one that breakthrough leaders will embrace and help both drive and shape.

o Plugging into the Circular Economy

If all this work on footprinting, new forms of P&L and ROI calculations, and big data analytics are to pay off in terms of real progress in relation to the Breakthrough Challenge, they must align with and support efforts to close the industrial loop and drive toward the emerging "circular economy." The aim here is to progressively uncouple wealth creation and welfare from natural resource consumption. This shift will require breakthrough leaders to work hard to assign realistic values to different forms of natural capital, accounting both for the depreciation of resources and the loss of biodiversity, as well as for the impact on other forms of capital.

Breakthrough change is most likely to be sparked — and to succeed — when we understand wider system dynamics. In their book *Bankrupting Nature*, Stockholm Resilience Centre director Johan Rockström and SRC board member Anders Wijkman argue that this challenge can be addressed only through a transformation of the entire economic system, including our financial markets.[19] A key element of a circular economy will be to design industrial systems that recycle and reuse materials wherever possible, and help phase out fossil fuels. This goal will best be achieved by adopting binding targets for resource efficiency, increasing taxes on the use of virgin materials, and lowering taxes on labor, coupled with national research policies that emphasize sustainable innovation and design.

One increasingly influential voice on the circular economy is that of the Ellen MacArthur Foundation. The foundation argues that "the circular economy provides a coherent framework for systems-level redesign and as such offers us an opportunity to harness innovation and creativity to enable a positive, restorative economy."[20]

This approach is built on a few key tenets: design out waste (that is, design nontoxic products and services that are meant to be repurposed); build resilience through diversity (design modular, versatile, and adaptive systems, products, and services); work toward using energy from renewable sources (design systems, products, and services that are meant to run on renewable resources); think in systems (understand how parts influence and interact with each other, and design systems, products, and services accordingly); and think in cascades (create and extract value by cascading products and materials through other applications).[21] The key point here, as the Ellen MacArthur Foundation points out, is that "a circular economy seeks to rebuild capital, whether this is financial, manufactured, human, social or natural."[22]

This goal is part and parcel of Plan B. Putting this into practice will require organizations to be accountable not just around their financial bottom lines but also around their wider social and environmental impacts. Note, however, that these impacts can be either positive or negative, so we increasingly see leading companies talking in terms of their ambitions to push toward "net positive" outcomes.

Kingfisher, Europe's largest home improvement retailer, manages its operations against fifty "Net Positive" targets, which are linked to management incentives.[23] A key part of the group's approach involves organizing internal conversations around critical elements of the agenda, including timber, energy, innovation, and communities. For example, Kingfisher's "Timber Conversation," held in fall 2013, brought together international experts in forest restoration, standards setting, social elements, and biodiversity accounting, and organizations such as FSC (Forest Stewardship Council), Greenpeace International, Rainforest Alliance, and WWF to explore how to develop a measurement system that is both practical and credible.[24]

A key component of the strategy involves informing and educating stakeholders, among them employees, customers, and suppliers. Kingfisher explains the business case for action: "by offering our customers energy-efficient products and the tools and materials for eco-retrofits and microgeneration projects, we can have a significant positive impact among the 6 million customers visiting our stores each week. This will give us access to a large new market for in-home energy efficiency, estimated to be worth around €70 billion across our key European markets by 2020. By harnessing closed-loop approaches we can tap into a cost-saving opportunity estimated to be worth around US$630bn per year across Europe."[25]

o   o   o

Such levels of transparency and engagement would have been almost unimaginable when the corporate transparency movement first began, but keeping up the pressure in this area will be core to Plan B, as will be education—an area we turn to next, in Chapter Eight.

8

Redefine Education

The B Team leaders see investments in education as the most important we will make in the coming decades. It's clear that despite their many defects, our education systems have succeeded in ways that would have been unimaginable a century or two ago. They are turning out some very bright young people ready to take on the world. In some ways, however, and particularly at the level of business schools, they have succeeded too well in indoctrinating students in conventional wisdom. Too many of the world's leading B-schools have been inculcating a single-bottom-line-focused agenda and linked set of values.

These monocular, one-dimensional values can be seen in C-suites around the world—and they are brought into even sharper focus in the minds and worldviews of most leading financial analysts. Optimists may note that a growing number of courses have picked up key elements of the people-planet-profit agenda, but too often they turn out specialists rather than leaders who can run major corporations or launch new ones. This problem has probably been clearest in the field of MBA education.

The MBA has been an astonishingly successful invention, effectively constituting a passport to the global C-suite. When the *Financial Times* polled MBA graduates from 153 business schools for its 2014 MBA rankings, it found that graduates from the one hundred top MBA programs were being paid twice what they had been five years earlier, despite the recessionary environment.[1] As a result, in recent decades, MBA education has been a boom industry.

At the time of this writing, 15,673 institutes worldwide offered business degrees at all levels. Still, as the *Financial Times* put it, "the question of whether many students are wasting their money on an irrelevant qualification is being more hotly debated than ever."[2] It is also worth noting that although many of those who now hold sway in the global C-suite have earned MBAs or have at least attended some B-school courses, most people in business around the world have neither been to B-school nor have an MBA or any other form of business degree.

Even some B-school professors admit that the reputation of the MBA qualification has been hard hit in recent times. "Traditional business education has not been without its problems," says Ioannis Ioannou, professor of strategy and entrepreneurship at London Business School (LBS). "Some people even blame business education for the collapse of the financial system, because of the excessive focus on short-term returns, and the sacrifice of the wider environment in order to achieve profits. And these are valid criticisms."

Although natural selection pressures are likely to spur further evolution in the B-school sector, the demand for their services seems secure. The "War for Talent," a term introduced by Steven Hankin of McKinsey & Company back in 1997, hasn't gone away. In Europe and the United States, for example, it is being driven by demographic shifts, with increasing demand for talent colliding with the reality of decreasing supply, as there are fewer post-baby-boom workers to replace retirees.

The proportion of employers reporting an increase in competition for well-qualified talent in the United Kingdom rose threefold from 20 percent in 2009 to 62 percent in 2013, according to the *CIPD/Hays Resourcing and Talent Planning Survey 2013*.[3] This annual survey, which examines resourcing and talent planning strategies across private, public, and voluntary sector organizations, found that six in ten organizations had experienced difficulties filling vacancies during the previous year — even in the midst of an economic downturn when the supply of unemployed or underemployed workers outstripped demand.

The pace of change in markets and business means that recruiters increasingly look not just for people who have learned but for those with an ability to continuing learning. The B Team leaders conclude that we must radically rethink education to ensure that it is an ongoing process throughout a person's working life. They also argue that instead of being treated as a niche subject, the Breakthrough Challenge must become the framework within which all business education is carried out. In short, tomorrow's B-schools must teach students to look well beyond business as usual and even change as usual.

In this context, ensuring a reasonable quantity of trained B-school students is only part of our task when it comes to redefining education. Few B-schools currently offer MBAs in sustainable business, although there are notable exceptions, including the Erb Institute at the University of Michigan, the MBA in sustainable management offered by the Presidio Graduate School, and the University of Exeter Business School One Planet MBA.[4]

Growing numbers of B-schools now offer options of one sort or another, but this poor showing from most schools sells students — and the future — short on one of the key issues for tomorrow's markets. Indeed, one well-known Insead professor we spoke to suggested that the B-school sector is overdue for a "product recall," updating past students on today's emerging realities and priorities.

○ Waking Up to the B-School Challenge

It is no accident that the issue of business education and training sits at the heart of Plan B. There is a critical need for breakthrough innovation in this sector. Feedback from those working at the cutting edge of business and education suggests, however, that there is still a huge hill to climb. Given the fact that it can take decades to clear out faculty members who think (and teach) in the old ways, business school deans must make tough decisions—rather than simply waiting for death and retirement to sort out the problem.

In the simplest terms, one of the weaknesses of business schools has been that they all too often churn out graduates who are poorly equipped to deal with issues other than those related directly to mainstream strategy, management, and finance. Still, nature abhors a vacuum, and one result of this area of weakness has been to spur new talent to break into the B-school world.

"I was often shocked about the ignorance and clumsiness of industry when faced with environmental questions," recalls Ulrich Steger, a former state government environment minister and member of the VW board, and later a professor at IMD, the Swiss business school. "For example, you saw very poor industry responses after the Schweizerhalle disaster in 1986, which massively polluted the Rhine. So when my political career ended in 1987, I jumped on the opportunity to assume the first professorial chair for environmental management in Europe."

Steger's early years in this area weren't always easy. Change rarely is. "My role model," he says with a twinkle, "was the woodpecker! Always banging away on the same spot, rapidly, time and again — without getting a headache." Today, Steger is retired, but the field he helped pioneer is opening up rapidly.

According to *Bloomberg Businessweek*, the list of prominent business schools that have driven through curriculum overhauls in recent years includes the Wharton School at the University of Pennsylvania; the Haas School of Business at the University of California, Berkeley; and Harvard Business School.[5] These schools have blazed new trails following the appointment of such deans as ethics scholar Nitin Nohria at Harvard and Sally Blount, an expert on the social impact of business, at the Kellogg School of Management at Northwestern University.

A number of issues — rather than any particular scandal or the collapse of financial institutions — precipitated these shifts away from a sole focus on financial matters to the wider world of environment, society, governance, and ethics. As one indication of the direction of change, recent surveys show that the "number of schools requiring a course in ethics, business in society, or a similar topic jumped from 34 percent in 2001 — before the Enron collapse — to 79 percent in 2011."[6]

Other positive signs also indicate encouraging changes in the way that at least some of today's leaders are rethinking B-school education. For instance, as already noted, corporate social responsibility and sustainability issues have long been seen as peripheral to business education, present, if at all, as options — for example, as half-day sessions on business ethics. At their worst, these can be a bit like the sort of sheep-dips used to coat farm animals with protection against insect infestations.

Rodolphe Durand, GDF SUEZ professor of strategy at HEC Paris, is one educator who sees the early stages of potentially seismic shifts in such areas. "Many top B-schools around the world consider these issues increasingly central," he says. "Entire courses are now developed and offered to students. Some organizations are created within existing faculties — and knowing how resistant to change faculty structures (and professors!) are, this is a strong signal of change."

Some schools, he explains, "create 'Business in Society' departments [as in the case of the Rotterdam School of Management, in The Netherlands], while others have their own research centers — at Stanford for instance, or more modestly the Society and Organizations Research Center that I launched here at HEC in the aftermath of the financial crisis. Also at HEC Paris, through the efforts of the Society and Organizations Research Center and the Grande Ecole's dean, we are thinking of making compulsory at least one sustainability course in the curriculum, plus one course per specialization (for example, strategy or marketing)."

To inspire, educate, and inform future generations of business leaders — and find solutions to the world's grand challenges — we will need new forms of strategy, innovation, investment, and management. Durand notes that "our markets are now increasingly mediated, with intermediary actors influencing dramatically the interplay between supply and demand. So the classical economic models do not work so well at the micro level. A better understanding of the interplay between such 'mediators' as rating agencies, accreditation agencies, the media off and online, and so on is crucial if we are to make sustainability issues part of the cognitive maps of current and future business leaders."

Part of what B-schools and other higher education institutions must change is the forms of management they teach, abandoning some classic models and adopting new methods that are better geared to tomorrow's risks and opportunities. "We need to integrate into our theory of competitive advantage a social and institutional component," Durand argues. "Once this is accomplished, we can offer a better model of why initiatives succeed or fail, and how to influence key mediators to give our new logic more legitimacy and, in the process, become more competitive."

No one senses the need for change more powerfully than the young people who are pondering what sort of education to invest in. More than ever, prospective graduate students are demanding programs that equip them to tackle environmental, social, and governance issues in the real world. The student-led global network Net Impact, for example, which celebrated its twenty-first year in 2013, had grown at that point to more than forty thousand members, with more than three hundred volunteer-led chapters driving impact on campus and on the job. Net Impact's 2013 *Business as UNusual* guide delivers what it calls the "inside scoop" on more than a hundred programs around the world. Each year, Net Impact surveys current MBA students, asking them to profile their program's curricula, activities, career services, and more. The result is the leading guide to the latest trends in sustainable business education and to MBA programs that address impact issues.

A growing proportion of the rising generation won't need to be forced to absorb the people-planet-profit agenda; doing so will be second nature. That said, worryingly, some survey evidence suggests that Gen Y is a still good deal less knowledgeable about sustainability issues than it will need to be. For instance, a recent study by Michigan State University and Deloitte found that Gen Y respondents showed a surprising lack of knowledge of green and sustainable technologies such as clean diesel, electric energy, and hybrid technology, which may lead to a "significant barrier to adoption" for such technologies.[7]

One of the toughest problems is that although some schools now pay greater lip service to some sustainability issues, few courses or MBA curricula do much to help shape an agenda that will enable future business leaders to embed the necessary perspectives, priorities, and processes into the day-to-day operations of their organizations and supply chains. By contrast, we must educate the rising generations of students in ways that fully integrate people-planet-profit considerations. This kind of education must increasingly flow through all phases, from undergrad to graduate programs to professional training and continuing education.

○ Changing the Relationship Between Business and B-Schools

Pressure to change business education also must be exerted from outside of academia. The recruiters and employers who come to B-schools looking for talent must push B-schools to change their research priorities and what they teach.

Evidence increasingly points to an ongoing shift in the attitudes of managers about what business schools should teach the students who will be their future hires. André van Heemstra, chairman of the steering group of the Dutch network of the UN Global Compact and formerly a board member and personnel director at Unilever, observes a fundamental shift. "When I started working for Unilever in 1970, the general advice I received from senior managers was to draw a sharp line between private and business life," he recalls. "The reason for this was that—on the job—one could well be confronted with situations in which one had to decide in a manner at odds with the principles one applied in one's personal life."

Of course, that was then. Things change. "I have witnessed the complete turnabout of this concept," van Heemstra notes. "Young managers today have an overriding urge to see their personal principles brought to life in their jobs. This is a very significant step forward—and the basis of an integrated sustainability understanding across a company. HR's challenge nowadays is to recruit young managers with principles that are aligned with the company's values." Tomorrow's leaders, as well as recruiters and employers, must work together to help catalyze this paradigm shift by building it into tomorrow's education.

The way business schools create the business cases they use to train future managers and leaders must also change. Jean-Pierre Jeannet, an emeritus professor both at IMD in Switzerland and Babson College in the United States, has tracked this shift. It is standard practice for business school case studies, which typically are the core of the business schools' offerings, to come attached with balance sheets and other financials. "I have yet to see a true and full-blown sustainability statement as part of any of these cases," he observes. Companies should be pressuring business schools to adapt their cases to the realities of multiple bottom lines, so that the graduates they hire are fully prepared and competitive.

The leading rank of business schools has been evolving fairly rapidly—though rarely fast enough for the more vocal students who want to bring their values to bear on the great challenges that their generation will have to confront and manage. One key to progress will be to convince recruiters and employers to seek out those students whose focus stretches beyond the financial bottom line to the sort of multidimensional mind-sets that will be critical to future success.

○ Meeting the Needs of Tomorrow's Students

The "let me through—I have an MBA" attitude of many business school alumni has often been at odds with the call for more effective stakeholder engagement in business. "It is always dangerous to generalize, but it is clear that there have been waves in terms of the people-and-planet agenda," observes Ulrich Steger. "The first ended in the oil crisis, the second peaked in the early 1990s and ended in the Asian financial crisis, and a third built through the middle of the last decade, ending with the Great Recession.

Similar waves could be seen in terms of the levels of student engagement and the readiness of faculty members to pick up these (at least for them) new topics."*

Now the student pressure seems to be building again, and young people are starting to demand changes in business school curricula. "More and more young people are part of this movement, which concerns today perhaps a sixth or even a fifth of the students I meet, up from a tiny fraction of this percentage a decade ago," reports HEC professor Rodolphe Durand. Others see the same trend: "Since I joined LBS in 2009, I have witnessed rapidly growing interest from the MBA and other degree program students, coupled with growing interest across cohorts, backgrounds, and nationalities," says Ioannis Ioannou.

These trends have important implications for how business school education will evolve. Mauro Guillén, an endowed professor in international management at the Wharton School, notes that "students are more and more interested in these issues, and they want to take classes, do internships, and do work in the area. However, in many cases, the good intentions clash with their need to secure a well-paying job to pay down their educational debt. Schools should have more loan forgiveness programs to help students who want to work in the CSR/ESG/sustainability space."

Guillén isn't alone in his observations of what today's students are looking for when they think about becoming tomorrow's leaders. Pamela Hartigan, director of the Skoll Centre for Social Entrepreneurship at Oxford University's Saïd Business School, agrees, noting that the most important deterrent for those

---

* In work beginning in 1994, John Elkington has tracked a series of societal pressure waves that have impacted governments, the media, business, and the financial markets. He has identified not three, but four, waves to date. The third, not mentioned in Ulrich Steger's account, focused on a rapidly evolving antiglobalization agenda; it peaked in 1999 (symbolized by the "Battle of Seattle," seeing major protests against the World Trade Organization) and was brought to a shuddering halt by the events of 9/11. See Volans, *Breakthrough: Business Leaders, Market Revolutions*, 2013. http://volans.com/wp-content/uploads/2013/02/Breakthrough_Volans_Final.pdf, 28–29.

wanting to pursue careers in sustainability "is the inordinate level of debt that these students graduate with. They are pressured to find positions that will help them liquidate the debt in a reasonable timescale. Then they get 'caught' in these jobs by family commitments, not happy but paid well."

Despite these challenges, Hartigan cites several key indicators of progress in the direction that today's business school students are headed, including growth in registration for classes on such subjects as social change, social innovation, social finance, impact measurement, and sustainable entrepreneurship. She also sees increased pressure from students for business schools to set up social venture incubators and accelerators. Behind it all, she says, is "a growing sense that business as usual is over, that the principles of sustainability have to be built into the business if it is to be viable in the longer term. The majority of student projects indicate a significant increase in those that incorporate sustainability principles into their business models. Those that venture to say they just want to make a lot of money are quickly chided by their peers."

Clearly, one of the pressing challenges in this area is finding ways to apply the lessons of tomorrow's sustainable business practices to today's real-world financial issues — that is, to find a way for young people to marry the two so that they better serve the people-planet-profit agenda. "I've been conducting an internship program for college graduates during the past two years to prepare them with the skills for sustainable business," says Ram Nidumolu, CEO of InnovaStrat, who previously served on the business school faculty at Santa Clara University and the University of Arizona.

> They have tremendous interest and passion for these topics, but no real understanding of how to convert these interests into marketable business skills. Graduates from liberal arts programs are especially passionate, but come

out of college disillusioned with business. After a three- to six-month internship program, they become very attractive to businesses and get recruited even in a tough market. The main problem that students and younger people face is that they are desperate to find a job in a terrible job market (50 percent-plus are unemployed, especially if they are liberal arts graduates), even as they retain a passion for doing something about sustainability. As a result, they often end up choosing the expedient over the passion-worthy.

Undeterred, business school students continue to push the envelope. One exciting student change initiative that we have already mentioned is Net Impact. Founded in 1993 as Students for Responsible Business (SRB), its inaugural conference was convened by thirteen graduate business students in the United States. Net Impact's mission today is "to empower a new generation to use their careers to drive transformational change in the workplace and the world."[8]

As an indicator of where student interest is currently focused, among the tracks at the 2013 Net Impact conference, held in Silicon Valley, were such themes as corporate impact, community development, entrepreneurship and social enterprise, environment and natural resources, sustainable food, and "tech for good." By contrast, the primary interest and focus a decade or two ago was on the impact of globalization and of the burgeoning New Economy.

Things are changing, as they always do. Many business schools are inching—and some leaping—toward new curricula that look beyond the financial bottom line to courses that better address the Breakthrough Challenge. They must do more. They must work with tomorrow's leaders to help redefine the social purpose of business. This means that breakthrough leaders, business school leaders, and students must work together to develop tools that will support the implementation of more sustainable ways of doing business, managing risks, and serving both existing and emerging human needs.

Meanwhile, as we noted at the outset, education increasingly goes beyond the preserve of MBA programs. Our education systems must fully embrace new forms of training and lifelong learning. This, in turn, will require a growing proportion of C-suite executives to rethink their own educational needs.

o Changing the Face of Executive Education

Redefining education is by no means restricted to the world of undergrads planning to move straight into MBA programs. Education, it is increasingly clear, must be a lifelong venture, especially for leaders of organizations that are moving along breakthrough trajectories. Thankfully, there is a growing market in various forms of executive education, particularly in the United States and Europe, with business schools and universities offering a range of courses touching on aspects of the Plan B agenda.

The even better news is that this growth is by no means restricted to the Western hemisphere. Some of the world's top schools, such as Harvard, Wharton, the University of Chicago, and Stanford, are offering programs in such places as China, India, Japan, and Saudi Arabia. As it becomes clear that major educational institutions like these are getting involved, the likelihood grows that their counterparts in the BRICS or MINT countries and elsewhere will follow suit.

One education leader who has worked in this space for more than twenty years is Polly Courtice, director of the University of Cambridge Programme for Sustainability Leadership (CPSL) and codirector of the Prince of Wales's Business & Sustainability Programme. Courtice has unusual insight into the ways in which C-suite executives have been engaged in learning over time.

"In the work we design for the C-suite," she says, "we have always had a fairly good spread of functional and business unit heads, including CEOs—particularly for initiatives like the Prince of Wales's Corporate Leaders Group. But CFOs have generally been underrepresented in many of our executive programs. And, partly in recognition of this, we launched a new CFO leadership program in 2013 with Accounting for Sustainability (A4S) and WBCSD."

She explains that priorities have changed significantly over time, both in terms of the issues covered as well as in the countries and regions most engaged over the past two decades. "When we set up our sustainability leadership seminars in the early 1990s, we mostly attracted senior executives from Europe—and the interest was very much in eco-efficiency and some social issues such as human rights," she says. "Today, participants are much more international, and their interest is more around putting sustainability into practice."

Meanwhile, organizations in almost every sector continue to face pressing issues such as a challenging economy and persistent unemployment. Although it is good news that international participants are taking a more active role in finding ways to merge sustainability and business, leaders in this field insist that the process has only just begun—and that there is still much work to be done. Courtice notes that although much of the focus in the European Union is now on creating jobs, there is also growing interest in Central and Eastern Europe in crafting policies to create green budgets and economies. Places like South Africa, too, are leading the way in innovative thinking around issues of energy and water as well as such social issues as employment, health, and social equity.

Although progress is certainly being made, and although many of those who have earned certificates in sustainability leadership are able to make positive impact in framing new strategies and engaging colleagues in the people-planet-profit agenda, many still face hurdles, particularly when it comes to incentivizing and rewarding staff in appropriate ways.

"Over the past ten years, we have seen the increasing incorporation of sustainability into business school curricula, research, and executive education," Courtice reports. "The U.S. has probably led Europe in this regard, certainly in terms of volume. However, in my view, business schools have failed to integrate sustainability in the ways required if we are to transform companies into institutions that can genuinely meet the great challenges of our time. The vast majority of sustainability programs at business schools appear to be bolt-on modules, and so far have done little to challenge or change mainstream teaching on the primacy of short-term shareholder value."

In some ways, what we have here is a chicken-and-egg dilemma: Which should come first? Should students agitate for change? Or should business schools build sustainability programs and hope the students will flock to them? Both supply and demand for sustainability leadership are growing. Students are, indeed, pushing for such courses, and some business schools are accommodating this need. However, we also need organizations of every ilk, across every sector, and in every country to put their shoulder to this wheel.

This will require organizations, students, recruiters, employers, and business schools and their faculties to think about education in decidedly different ways, moving beyond whiteboards and PowerPoint presentations to methods that take students out of static classrooms and into real-world situations where they can see firsthand the evidence of breakdown, the dynamics of business-as-usual and change-as-usual processes, and the impact that breakthrough-oriented leaders can have in driving solutions to the Breakthrough Challenge.

o Rediscovering Experiential Learning

If we are to alert the leaders of today and tomorrow to wider realities, one of the best ways is to get them out into the real world. For some students, interest in this agenda is something they were born with. For others, there was a moment when they were forced to engage with a different reality. For yet others, it is something that gradually caught their attention as they read the academic literature and followed the media — or, in the case of faculty members, as their students sought to do internships with organizations working in related fields.

One of the most interesting trends is the growing interest of at least some business leaders in offering their people experiential learning opportunities. Barclays CEO Antony Jenkins is one participant in the trend for C-suite executives to involve their top team in experiential learning processes. Barclays, the U.K.-based banking group, worked through a massive crisis that stripped away many key members of its leadership team. Significantly, an independent inquiry had concluded that astronomical pay and a culture of entitlement had led to what it called an "ethical vacuum" at the bank.[9] When, shortly after taking over as CEO, Jenkins first announced his "Project Transform" — designed to make Barclays the go-to bank for all its shareholders, rebuild its reputation, and increase profits — the company's shares climbed almost 10 percent. Not long after, however, Barclays announced profit losses and came under intense pressure, again, when regulators insisted that it meet tighter leverage ratios earlier than expected.

Fully committed to Project Transform despite the bank's wider challenges, Jenkins took top team members to Kenya as part of a program to see firsthand the bank's impact around the world. "The social impact of Barclays has long been central to my leadership approach," he explains. "Not only consideration of mitigating the negative, but more importantly how the business can have a positive social, as well as commercial, impact. In fact, I believe there is a symbiotic connection between having strong values and value creation, which is core to whether a business can enjoy truly sustainable success."

Given that culture change processes often take decades, it is too early to judge where this process will take Barclays and other organizations that are moving in this direction. Nevertheless, it is increasingly clear that types of education that happen well beyond the classroom walls will be crucial as we begin to tackle the huge behavioral and cultural barriers that loom ahead.

The evidence suggests that profound cultural awakenings can follow such experiences as being taken into the heart of a Nairobi slum or a Mumbai landfill site. When entire teams share the same experience, the results can include new forms of learning and bonding—coupled with an intense appreciation not only of social or environmental problems previously masked by the urgency of everyday life but also of some of the linked market opportunities that are now emerging.

Jenkins has been a leading supporter of Leaders' Quest, an organization that specializes in such learning journeys. Lindsay Levin, founder and managing partner, argues that experiential learning is invaluable—and likely to become more so. "We believe that the most powerful learning in life typically comes through experience and immersion, rather than teaching or debate," she explains. "We bring people together to learn from the unfamiliar, to ask tough questions about life and the way they (and we) choose to live it, and to recognize the capacity they have to improve the world around them. At its core, Leaders' Quest is about being as much as doing, and the search for a larger sense of individual, and collective purpose."

Approaches like this are very much in keeping with Plan B, teaching individuals to look well beyond the financial bottom line and thus helping them understand the bigger picture and the implications for their businesses. Organizations like Leaders' Quest, which strives to "shift the possible," open the door for people to learn about themselves and the world in new ways. "We think of the work we do as 'holding a space' for people to experience themselves and the world anew," Levin says. "Quests, and the support we provide around them, are about deepening consciousness of our human interdependence with one another and with all of life, and awakening a sense of profound connection in people who often have spent very little time thinking and feeling in this way."

Of course, not everyone will immediately and willingly buy in to the notion of experiential learning. For some leaders, it will seem too soft, too intangible. Many of today's leaders will question how to measure the ROI for experiential learning. Sometimes, however, learning need not boil down to numbers. "Clients often, and understandably, ask us how we measure impact," Levin says. "Once we're under way they almost never do. The obsession with boiling everything down to metrics has squeezed out so much of what matters most in life, and the inner shift we are seeking to help people make is not easily measurable in a conventional sense."

This is set to become an increasingly competitive space. The Hong Kong–based Global Institute for Tomorrow is another emerging player. Founder Chandran Nair takes executives from companies like BASF and NEC to visit and work with NGOs and social enterprises across Asia. "Rather than get McKinsey to do a report for $5 million," he says, "why not take your best 25–50 people from around the world and we'll facilitate a program where the traditional biases [of western capitalism and business school thinking] will become less obvious."[10]

o Helping Today's Faculty Teach Tomorrow's Leaders

In the end, the make-or-break aspect of business school responses will be the extent to which the faculty members embrace the new challenges and build them directly into their courses and cases. "There is both interest and excitement at LBS about this," says Ioannou. "This is illustrated by the multiple initiatives, commitments, and engagements the school has undertaken in recent years."

LBS is, for example, one of the three hub universities for the Schmidt-MacArthur Fellowship, designed to promote innovative thinking on the circular economy by exceptional students from all over the world. LBS also is a partner institution for Deloitte's Social Innovation Pioneers, which supports high-potential social innovators. In addition, incoming MBA cohorts engage in a theme centered around "shaping a sustainable future," kicked off by leaders like David Blood of Generation Investment Management, whose credibility partly reflects the fact that he formerly ran the asset management side of Goldman Sachs.

A growing number of B-schools are opening up and inviting in such leaders from the Plan B world, either as lecturers or as visiting, adjunct, or even full professors. The business media have been tracking this trend, spotlighting the fact that B-schools are inviting real-world leaders into their classrooms to discuss real-world issues. Even better is the news that, as the *Financial Times* recently reported, "This is particularly true in the area of sustainability, where schools have been racing to meet the voracious appetite among students for content on issues such as climate change, resource efficiency and poverty mitigation."[11]

Among the examples used to illustrate this welcome trend is professor Bruce Usher, who from 2002 to 2009 was chief executive of EcoSecurities, a carbon credit and consulting group who now teaches at Columbia Business School. Usher is codirector of the Social Enterprise Programme and an executive-in-residence at Columbia, where he has been an adjunct professor in finance since 2002. As such, the *Financial Times* noted, "he is one of a growing number of former chief executives hired by business schools to teach MBA students how to build environmental and social considerations into corporate strategy."[12]

Meanwhile, at Case Western Reserve University's Weatherhead School of Business, Roger Saillant, former chief executive of Plug Power, a fuel-cell power company, got the job as executive director of the Fowler Centre for Sustainable Value. Michael Crooke, former Patagonia chief executive, has been a full-time faculty member at Pepperdine University's Graziadio School of Business, where he oversees sustainability teaching. At Copenhagen Business School, Mads Øvlisen, former chief executive of Novo Nordisk, the health care company that rechartered itself around the triple-bottom-line agenda, has served as adjunct professor of corporate social responsibility.

Increasingly, business schools and their faculties are waking up to the fact that today's breakthrough leaders have cutting-edge ideas about how to future-proof business. Students, meanwhile, must understand not only that advancing this agenda is possible but also that there are leaders who are successfully implementing and promoting it today.

Consider the example of Gail Whiteman, professor of sustainability, management, and climate change at the Rotterdam School of Management. Her recent employment history underscores the broadening overlap between these different worlds. Also a professor-in-residence at the World Business Council for Sustainable Development, Whiteman sums up the agenda that tomorrow's B-schools will have to embrace: "B-schools must in their programs include topics such as the 'One-Earth Paradigm,' the growing importance of planetary boundaries, the business case for sustainability, the new Low Carbon Economy, the opportunities to be found at the bottom of the pyramid, and the environmental profit and loss approach," she explains. "Young, talented people need not only to understand tomorrow's bottom line but also must be able to articulate in a multistakeholder dialogue the issues and required solutions for a postconsumerist economy."

Critically, such experts and educators now believe, tomorrow's business leaders will need to develop the entrepreneurial skills and enthusiasm to support innovators as they seek to break through to more sustainable forms of value creation, a need that has massive implications for the future of business education and training, wherever it may be offered.

○ Reengineering Tomorrow's B-Schools

So, given the growing evidence that students and executives want better education and training, why are today's business schools not doing more? Many leaders in the field see an obvious answer: to allow for — and drive — change, business schools must be rated and ranked in significantly different ways.

"Business schools need to band together to work on revamping the ranking criteria that have enslaved too many of them into pursuing the same curriculum, although what society expects from business — and what students seek — have changed profoundly," says Pamela Hartigan, who heads the Skoll Center for Social Entrepreneurship at the Saïd Business School, Oxford. "For example, one critical criterion in the rankings is the salary level of recent graduates. But entrepreneurial ventures, whether for profit or not for profit, as well as the sorts of opportunities available in the growing supporting ecosystem, are not in a position to pay salaries that can compete with mainstream banks and consulting firms. Result: a totally skewed ranking system that is not responding to what the world needs now or in the future."

Probably the best-known initiative in this field to date is Beyond Grey Pinstripes, a research survey and alternative ranking of business schools. Like the Net Impact surveys, this spotlights innovative full-time MBA programs that are leading the way in the integration of issues concerning social and environmental stewardship into the curriculum.[13] The idea behind the work is that these schools "are preparing students for the reality of tomorrow's markets by equipping them with the social, environmental, ethical and economic perspectives required for business success in a competitive and fast changing world." The scale of the task underscores the complexity of the challenge. Some twelve thousand courses and faculty research abstracts, plus four thousand examples of institutional support such as extracurricular programs and joint degree offerings, were collected from 149 participating schools.

The roots of the program run deep. In 1998, the World Resources Institute (WRI) created *Grey Pinstripes with Green Ties*, a report that examined the inclusion of environmental management topics in thirty-seven MBA programs. The following year, WRI partnered with the Aspen Institute's Business and Society Program (Aspen BSP) to balance the report by examining MBA programs for the teaching of social impact management. This led to the creation of the Beyond Grey Pinstripes initiative.

Over time, the resulting research has been used by tens of thousands of students, academics, and major corporations. The website contains detailed information about more than 150 global MBA programs. A key goal is to "raise the bar by challenging business schools to incorporate social and environmental impact management topics into their curricula." In parallel, there is a sense that it is important to stimulate conversations in the B-school world, on the basis that "real change only comes after students, faculty, administrators and business leaders begin to discuss these issues."[14]

As today's students become tomorrow's leaders, they will need to get a better grip on the intricacies of creating value (some would call it blended value, others shared value) across the triple-bottom-line agenda. From classroom to conference room to boardroom, they will need to understand that breakthrough leadership must move well beyond managing profits and measuring the standard financial metrics. Students and faculty members alike must get out of the classroom and interact with real-world leaders who are finding ways to break through to the "future quo." Further, what is true for students and faculty members will be increasingly true for anyone working in the private, public, and citizen sectors.

o o o

In looking forward to a shift toward (Plan B) business schools, The B Team leaders foresee new uses of MOOCs (massive open online courses), endowed chairs and professorships focusing on the Plan B agenda, and even totally new educational institutions. They also see a growing role for nature in the classroom. In the end, the impetus must come from the students who pay for the courses, the businesses that employ them, and the deans and professors who are determined to ensure that their schools are fit for purpose in the coming decades. One emerging aspect of tomorrow's business education will involve learning from nature's model — and from experts in the rapidly evolving field of biomimicry. That's the focus of the next chapter.

9

Learn from Nature's Model

If we are to succeed in making business sense out of the Break-through Challenge, we need not just different priorities but also new types of thinking about how value is best created and distributed. Many of the necessary ideas will be developed well outside the box — that is, outside the walls and confines of our incumbent companies, industries, disciplines, and mind-sets.

In that context, anyone looking for powerful insights into tomorrow's technologies and business models would be well advised to turn to someone — or something — that has a long track record of developing breakthrough innovations. Given that nature has been doing just this for several billion years, that's where a growing number of innovators and entrepreneurs have been turning for inspiration on how the future can be both radically different and radically better.

Our planet is brimming with clues as to how new forms of value might be created. Humankind has learned countless valuable lessons from the natural world, often by studying ways in which nature has solved some of the intractable challenges we have encountered along the way. Think of the first people to harness the seemingly miraculous—if dangerous—power of fire to cook food, keep predators at bay, warm caves, and pull families and tribes together in convivial groups during the unsettling dark hours. Think of those who fashioned the first wheels, very likely by extrapolating from the use of trunks and logs as rollers. Think of those who used remedies based on tree bark, including bark from the willow and the cinchona tree—the original source of now ubiquitous medicines like aspirin and quinine. Or think of those who worked out how to produce a wide range of fermentation products, among them bread, beer, wine, and early antibiotics.

Today, the rapidly emerging field of biomimicry—the imitation of the models, elements, and systems of nature for the purpose of solving complex human problems—is shifting this approach into overdrive. The accelerating hunt for physical, chemical, and, above all, biological and ecological clues to tomorrow's inventions and innovations is becoming one of the most exciting areas of science, technology, and design.

Simultaneously, however, time is running out for many of the species that have accompanied us on the evolutionary journey to date, a point that was underscored by former WWF International director-general Jim Leape. Like other scientists, he believes that we are seeing the "Sixth Great Extinction," with fully half of the world's species likely to go extinct over the next hundred years. "The most important cause is the widespread destruction of natural habitats, both terrestrial and aquatic, in particular for the production of food and fiber—plus the extraction of other resources and the spreading of human settlements," Leape explains. "A second, and rapidly increasing driver of biodiversity loss is climate change."

It may be too late to turn things around, but that doesn't mean there isn't any hope. "Obviously we can't go back to the state of nature fifty or a hundred years ago," Leape acknowledges.

"The inertia in the system, not least the climate system, means that we are destined to experience significant further change. But it is not too late to make a big difference in the outcomes, to shift humanity on to a much more benign path—and to conserve much of our natural heritage."

Perhaps, too, biomimicry can give us a better sense of the value of what we are now losing—while at the same time helping evolve the technologies, the economic and business models, and above all the mind-sets needed to create businesses, economies, and societies that help protect what we have left.

o Probing the Three Levels of Biomimicry

So where to find the clues to where biomimicry may take us? Ask Janine Benyus, the world's leading champion of biomimicry, what it's all about, and she responds by sketching out three main domains of activity.[1]

The first level is the mimicking of natural form, she says. "For instance, you may mimic the hooks and barbules in an owl's feather to create a fabric that opens anywhere along its surface. Or you can imitate the frayed edges that grant the owl its silent flight." Copying the design of feathers is just the beginning, of course, not least because it is far from guaranteed to offer immediate solutions to sustainability challenges.

At the second level, the focus shifts to deeper forms of biomimicry, involving the mimicking of the natural processes that actually make a feather. "The owl feather self-assembles at body temperature without toxins or high pressures, by way of nature's chemistry," Benyus explains. "The unfurling field of green chemistry attempts to mimic these benign recipes."

The third level is the mimicking of natural ecosystems. "The owl feather is gracefully nested—it's part of an owl that is part of a forest that is part of a biome that is part of a sustaining biosphere."

In the same way, any owl-inspired fabric or material must be part of a larger economy that works to restore rather than deplete the earth and the communities in which people live.

To contribute to the wider trajectory toward sustainable capitalism, biomimicry will need to evolve in the right sort of cultural and even environmental context. Benyus stresses that if a company makes a bioinspired fabric with green chemistry, but still has workers weaving it in a sweatshop, loading it onto pollution-spewing trucks, and then shipping it long distances, the whole process has missed the point. "To mimic a natural system," she says, "you must ask how each product fits in — is it necessary, is it beautiful, is it part of a nourishing food web of industries, and can it be transported, sold, and reabsorbed in ways that foster a forestlike economy?"

Nature's model offers a rich wellspring of innovative ideas. Among linked concepts are cradle-to-cradle design (promoted by Bill McDonough and Michael Braungart), a biomimetic approach to the design of products and systems; industrial symbiosis (as developed at Denmark's Kalundborg industrial complex), a "web of materials and energy exchanges among companies";[2] and, as already mentioned, the circular economy (championed, among others, by the Ellen MacArthur Foundation).

This is an area that sees a constant flow of new ideas and new terms. McDonough and Braungart, for example, also have developed a number of other business memes, among them eco-effectiveness, the triple top line, and upcycling. In contrast to downcycling, the process whereby materials move to progressively lower-grade applications through recycling, upcycling does what nature does, turning waste materials into higher-added-value goods.

The B Team leaders see nature's models as holding almost infinite potential in just about every Plan B priority area. Champions of the approach sense that nature's teachers are hidden in plain sight all around us. "Camel's nostrils are miracles of heat exchange and water-recovery engineering," notes British architect Michael Pawlyn.[3] "We are currently looking at cuttlebone and bird skulls to help design more efficient concrete structures for office buildings. The combustion chamber in the abdomen of a bombardier beetle mixes two high explosives from fuel tanks with valves that open and close two hundred times a second—it is being studied in order to develop needle-free medical injections, more efficient fuel injection systems, and more effective fire extinguishers."

Like a growing number of breakthrough pioneers around the world, Pawlyn is passionate about biomimicry and its potential to drive transformative change. Indeed, some people now see biomimicry as "the business link to biodiversity."[4] Others see the discipline as a keystone element in what they call "natural capitalism," which aims to protect, grow, and learn from "earth's natural resources and the ecological systems that provide vital life-support services to society and all living things."[5] However we choose to think about it, the fascinating thing about biomimicry is that its lessons can apply to just about any aspect of our lives.

○ Grasping the Ultimate Bottom Line

Perhaps the greatest gift biomimicry offers is that it helps us see our world through powerful new lenses. In the process, it can help us think differently about how we define and respond to the Breakthrough Challenge generally—and to tomorrow's bottom line in particular.

As we experiment with biomimicry, we can expect a totally new type of business school case to evolve. For example, consider the chef who fell in love with a fish, a story told in American chef Dan Barber's TED talk.[6] He recalls his visits both to a fish farm where 30 percent of the fish-feed was chicken waste and, in stark contrast, to a vast wetland aquaculture site in Spain—where a key indicator of success is the pinkness of the bellies of the flamingos that commute extraordinary distances to consume 20 percent of the semifarmed fish. For many fish farmers this would be unacceptable loss, but those who run the site see this as a reasonable price to pay for wider ecosystem health.

In working out the business model for their restaurant in New York, the Barber brothers described their "ultimate bottom line" as the health of the soils they farm. Learning from nature's model can benefit the people-planet-profit agenda in ways that are profoundly complementary to other Plan B priorities, among them the growing interest in the circular economy (discussed in Chapter Seven).

Indeed, one of Michael Pawlyn's declared ambitions is to turn linear consumption models into cycles, with waste used to fuel another cycle of activity, mimicking the interdependency of ecosystems. Take the Eden Project in Cornwall, where he worked as a lead architect, and which is now a globally known example of the biomimicry approach. The design of the site's biomes was influenced by gossamer-thin — but remarkably strong — dragonfly wings. Here nature led the way in the design of the largest greenhouse in the world, an efficient, sustainable project that in its first three years contributed £500 million to the local economy.[7]

"In hindsight, our major bottom line was regeneration," explains the project's founder, Sir Tim Smit. This involved the repositioning of the county of Cornwall, which is geographically remote and economically troubled, through the use of iconic architecture and a new approach to science. By regenerating a derelict clay mine and transforming it into a place of fertile abundance, Eden provided a massive green boost to the regional economy. "Independent professionals conservatively estimate our contributions of new wealth to Cornwall at £1.3 billion," says Smit. "Some would call that a positive externality! In fact, it represents a monster return on our total state, lottery, and EU investment of some £100 million, against a total investment of some £144 million."

To be successful, tomorrow's solutions developed using biomimicry must also be shaped by tomorrow's ethics. This will require a major shift in the way we view the natural world. "Right now we tell ourselves that the earth was put here for our use, that we are at the top of the pyramid when it comes to earthlings," is the way Janine Benyus puts it.

> But of course this is a myth. We've had a run of spectacular luck, but we are not necessarily the best survivors over the long haul. We are not immune to the laws of natural selection, and if we overshoot the carrying capacity of the earth, we will pay the consequences. Practicing ethical biomimicry will require a change of heart. We will have to climb down from our pedestal and begin to see ourselves as simply a species among species, as one vote in a parliament of thirty million [other species]. When we accept this fact, we start to realize that what is good for the living earth is good for us as well.

Maintaining a continuous awareness of nature's ultimate bottom line will be a critically important factor in our efforts to tackle the Breakthrough Challenge and deliver Plan B. Biomimicry by its very nature "is an innovation method that seeks sustainable solutions by emulating nature's time-tested patterns and strategies, e.g., a solar cell inspired by a leaf. The goal is to create products, processes, and policies—new ways of living—that are well-adapted to life on earth over the long haul."[8]

o Innovating Like Nature

From Velcro (whose design was suggested by the way that weed burrs snag in a dog's fur) to passive cooling, self-healing plastics, and artificial photosynthesis, business has created some very cool products thanks to biomimicry.[9] Like Velcro, some of these products will find their way into our everyday lives, to the point where we will become oblivious to their existence.

Today, leading businesses are already profiting from this deeply rooted wisdom. Lufthansa, for example, is learning from nature's model, devising ways to tweak its existing technologies to better align with the people-planet-profit agenda. For example, two Lufthansa Airbus A340-300s recently took part in a special mission. Eight innovative test patches had been placed on the fuselage and leading edge of the wings of each Airbus. According to the company, "the aim of the research is to test the durability of a surface coating for aircraft that mimics shark skin under real-life flying conditions. The riblets that cover the entire skin of fast-swimming sharks reduce turbulent vortices and the drag they cause. This diminishes surface resistance when moving at speed. Thanks to a new technique developed by the Fraunhofer Institute in Bremen, shark-skin structures can be embossed into aircraft paints. According to the latest research findings, this aerodynamic surface could reduce fuel consumption by about 1 percent."[10]

That may not sound like a lot, but spread over the working life of an aircraft, it could add up to some very attractive savings in fuel costs. In the process of such early experiments, companies like Lufthansa are discovering that nature offers powerful lessons about how to work more efficiently, more sustainably, and (if things go well) more profitably. Working with the grain of nature will allow tomorrow's breakthrough leaders to innovate in ways that perform well against every dimension of the triple bottom line.

Nature's models provide insights suitable not only for designing and engineering materials and products; increasingly they also will find applications in designing and operating systems.

As Hans Schürmann of Siemens notes, there is much to be learned from complex systems, such as weather and biochemical processes in the body. Nature's complex systems can provide insights into a number of human issues. Says Schürmann, "Today we know that many processes in power generation, manufacturing, traffic guidance systems, and logistics can be managed by neural networks that function in a manner similar to the way nerves link up in the brain. The big advantage here is that such artificial neural networks can learn from examples generated in real time and respond flexibly to changed conditions. [This] will make it possible to access knowledge in a totally new way and also enable the development of new business models and services."[11]

○ Gaining Buy-In for Biomimicry

As the buzz grows, biomimicry is making its way into some of the world's most innovative R&D labs. How can we inject some of the emerging insights into the thinking of corporate boards and the global C-suite? Time and again, the uncomfortable fact is that many new developments in science, technology, and business are initially dismissed as crazy. To recall one of George Bernard Shaw's maxims: reasonable people adapt themselves to the world; unreasonable people attempt to adapt the world to themselves; therefore, all progress depends on unreasonable people.[12]

Today's short-term-obsessed leaders may think it unreasonable or unfeasible to embrace biomimicry in the ways we've described. Nevertheless, the discipline clearly holds the seeds of a radically better future if applied properly to support the drive toward sustainable technologies, businesses, and economies. Indeed, innovative organizations report that learning from nature's model has paid dividends in more ways than one—despite initial pushback from some of their own people, including members of their top team.

"When we started Mission Zero, people thought we'd gone mad. But it's proved to be the most important decision we've taken." So says Nigel Stansfield, senior director for product design and innovation of InterfaceFLOR, the world's largest designer and maker of carpet tile, and a leading corporate champion of the benefits of learning from nature's model. Mission Zero is a company-wide initiative that moves the organization away from a "take-and-waste" approach toward a model much closer to the principles of a circular economy that measures and accounts for its footprint from A to Z.

This shift toward closed-loop design and biomimicry has led to tremendous — and eminently measurable — benefits for the company: "Since 1996, InterfaceFLOR has reduced its manufacturing waste to landfill by 75%," the company reports. "Net greenhouse gas emissions have been cut by 82%, water usage by 75% and energy consumption per unit of output by half. All energy used in its European manufacturing sites is renewable, as is 27% of global energy consumption. Mission Zero has enabled the company to save more than $372 million in avoided waste costs."[13]

InterfaceFLOR has worked with both Biomimicry 3.8 and David Oakey Designs on new approaches that apply lessons from the natural world to the design and production of carpet tiles. By asking how nature designs a floor, the company developed its i2 line of products, including Entropy, one of its most popular products. This was inspired by the "organized chaos" of the forest floor. Then there are the company's TacTiles, inspired by the many examples of adhesion without glue in nature: they use small adhesive squares to connect carpet without the need for traditional glues.

InterfaceFLOR's Mission Zero initiative is just one example of the ways that a company can successfully bring its people on board in this area. Companies large and small are waking up to the lessons nature can teach. GE, for example, has studied the structure of seashells to devise new ways to mimic their architecture in building gas turbine blades.[14] Qualcomm has turned to butterflies to exploit the phenomenon of optical interference to improve the displays in e-readers.[15] Sprint, Procter & Gamble, and NASA are just a few of the other organizations now looking to biomimicry as sources of inspiration for sustainable innovation.

"The companies that we're working with now are much more open," Benyus reports. "Instead of just tweaking their original products, they're saying to us, 'Let's have a completely new look at this.'"[16]

Used in the right way, biomimicry brings new insights and new ways of thinking at precisely the moment in history when the Breakthrough Challenge entails rethinking, rebooting, redesigning, and reengineering. We're not just talking about learning from nature's model in such fields as design or architecture.

Take Craig Venter, founder of Synthetic Genomics and more recently the J. Craig Venter Institute, who sees synthetic biology as a powerful way of learning from nature and creating radically new solutions and technologies to address challenges like global warming.[17] His team uses ultrapowerful computers and new forms of gene sequencing not just to study organisms but also to work out how to create totally new ones, unknown to science. In this quest, his institute has uncovered more than sixty million genes and thousands of novel protein families from organisms found in seawater. It has also sequenced microbial flora found in a range of "human environments," among them the vagina, oral cavity, and gut. With massive volumes of data likely to be generated, some of these organisms and genes will offer crucial insights into how we can evolve radically different technologies.

Much of this will be highly controversial, as the introduction of new technologies often is. However, the thing about nature is that it has tried out a lot of stuff over immense timescales; a great number of these "trials" have bombed, but what survives does so because it works—in multiple dimensions. Nature has much to teach us, clearly, and one thing it can do is to stretch our time horizons. This is perhaps the most important of The B Team challenges, to which we turn in Chapter Ten.

10

Keep the Long Run in Mind

Time horizons are central to The B Team agenda. Too many organizations have focused for too long on short-term horizons in which quarterly earnings have reigned supreme. Chances are that this era will end sooner than many people imagine—as such periods tend to—and that the pendulum will once again begin to swing in favor of businesses that think and invest longer term.

Nevertheless, business remains too focused on the short term, and Dominic Barton, global managing director of McKinsey & Company, has joined forces with Mark Wiseman, president and CEO of the Canada Pension Plan Investment Board (CPPIB), to warn that "the tyranny of short-termism" is currently gaining an even stronger grip on the global C-suite.

When McKinsey and CPPIB surveyed more than one thousand board members and C-suite executives worldwide, no less than 63 percent of the respondents said that the pressure to generate short-term returns had increased over the previous five years.[1] Four-fifths (79 percent) felt especially pressured to show strong financial performance over a period of two years or less.

Nearly half (44 percent) said they were using a time horizon of less than three years in setting their strategy. At the same time, 86 percent admitted that they felt that they should be using a longer time horizon—and that to do so would help strengthen financial returns and boost innovation.

Shifting in this way, Barton and Wiseman conclude, will depend on the financial sector, in particular on "large asset owners such as pension funds, mutual funds, insurance firms, and sovereign wealth funds. If they adopt investment strategies aimed at maximizing long-term results, then other key players—asset managers, corporate boards, and company executives—will likely follow suit."

It is certainly true that much of today's capitalist system seems focused on efficiency and narrowly defined productivity, ignoring longer-term existential threats linked to a booming global population and a natural resource base that is increasingly straining at the seams. Breakthrough innovation, by contrast, is often anything but efficient: it disrupts, it can undermine short-term productivity, and it can struggle for ages to get off the ground. When it does take flight, though, everything changes (eventually).

A key skill for tomorrow's leaders will be to get a better grip on where the future is likely to take us, and on what it will take to evolve our global economic system to make it fit for the coming decades. How likely is this to happen? One recent long-term system change project was summarized in the Club of Rome's report, *2052: A Global Forecast for the Next Forty Years*. Its author, Jørgen Randers, a professor of climate strategy at the BI Norwegian Business School, has been a leading figure in sustainable development for forty years, since he coauthored the *Limits to Growth* study. Randers has reluctantly concluded that the system changes now needed to ensure true sustainability may not happen—at least on the necessary scale and in the required timescales.[2]

Randers and his team are concerned that the 2030s will see worldwide revolution, just as the 1840s did in Europe, in part driven by disenfranchised young people. However accurate or inaccurate such forecasts may prove to be, they underscore the fact that we are coming up against a set of generational, even civilizational, challenges. The issue is what change-oriented business leaders can do about it—and how they can build long-term thinking into their planning and investment programs.

The B Team leaders are alert to both the opportunities and challenges of focusing on the long term. They advocate creating and supporting longer-term frameworks for capitalism, markets, and business. They also stress that it will be crucial to work toward this goal collectively, sharing approaches and best practices so that other organizations can make similar changes in their own operations and processes—and avoid at least some of the pitfalls along the way.

The delivery of Plan B will require that breakthrough leaders consider a list of key questions, including the following:

- How do you make business more long term?
- How do you account for natural capital?
- How do you make natural capital—and social capital—part of your guidance for investors?
- How do you build planetary boundaries into your operating model?

Unilever CEO Paul Polman reports that his organization is already at work on tackling a number of these long-term challenges:

> We are moving our industry globally to natural alternatives to HFC/CFC refrigerants. We are working hard to address issues of deforestation in Indonesia and sustainable food supply in Africa. We've worked with the

U.K. government on carbon reporting as a first step to compulsory reporting and in Mexico on environmental reporting, trying to create critical mass around these projects. And, to take another example, it took a lot of effort from us to change the tax regulations on sustainable palm oil in India. We should be able to say to ourselves in two, three, or five years that we are in a better place because we acted together than we would have been had we acted alone.

○ Expanding the C-Suite Time Horizon

Although it is good news that such CEOs are making progress, it will take more than a handful of breakthrough leaders to advance the paradigm shift that is needed. "A lot of people are discussing these topics, but CEOs feel very exposed in taking a lead," Polman warns. "There's a real problem of scale. Any one of us doing what we are doing alone—which can be very good, by the way—is not creating the critical mass needed to drive impact on a global scale. We are at the point, both for humanity and for future generations, where we urgently need to create projects that have impact at that scale. We must invite politicians and NGOs to participate, but we cannot wait for them."

Prior to moving to Unilever, Polman was a senior executive at archrival Nestlé. Let's look back to where he came from. Peter Brabeck-Letmathe of Nestlé is an example of a former CEO (now chairman) who has woken up to the strategic importance of the wider societal agenda, first driving organizational changes and then moving on to wider advocacy.[3] Among other things, he has been deeply involved in the water security debate.

Given that Nestlé was the company where the shared value movement first took root, Brabeck-Letmathe has a useful perspective into the challenges of integrating multiple forms of value into the corporate balance sheet. Senior leaders, he argues, must focus on long-term sustainable business goals and practices, because long-term business thinking leads directly to creating shareholder value, together with real social progress. "Interest is growing in this approach, but many barriers remain to long-term thinking—not the least of which is the reporting of quarterly earnings and a focus on short-term profit maximization."

Corporate executives must be incentivized to think longer term within the business, and they also must be pushed to make the right moves through an evolving external regulatory framework that gives them the confidence and support to do so. "This must involve boards of directors changing executive compensation plans," Brabeck-Letmathe argues, "investors rewarding long-term shareholder value creation, and public policy changes which help to focus companies on the long term. It also takes CEOs who have the strength to simultaneously resist an exclusive focus on the short term, creating acceptable short-term profits while executing long-term plans for sustainable shareholder value."

At Nestlé, these agendas have been spurred from the top by the chairman, the CEO, and the executive board. Implementation is pushed across functional and geographic sectors, from R&D throughout the value chain to sales, marketing, and consumer communications. This kind of company-wide engagement is never easy, but is crucial when it comes to teaching organizations to think long term.

Typically, a key part of the CEO's role is to deliver the goals and targets agreed on with the board by inspiring, directing, and supporting fellow C-suite executives. There has been a rapid proliferation of C-suite roles over time, including the chief sustainability officer and even, linking back to the well-being agenda, the occasional chief spiritual officer. Few would deny, however, that the second most powerful (and sometimes the most powerful) person in many C-suites is the chief financial officer (CFO).

Unfortunately, CFOs are often seen as barriers to change, overly focused on short-term financial issues. Former IMD professor Ulrich Steger speaks of CFOs as having been at the top of his "Stubbornness Index." One Australian chief sustainability officer we talked to spoke for many when he described his company's CFO as a "toughie." Some people, off the record, were less polite. Anyone who is skeptical about the prospect of the current generation of CFOs deciding of their own free will to help save the world may be right to worry. Research suggests that most CFOs tend to be nervous about bringing these issues to their boards, believing that the available data are not yet sufficiently robust or reliable or that colleagues may see the quantification of the related risks and opportunities as spurious or even as borderline unethical.

CFOs, however, must now play an increasingly active role in driving progress. They need not only to speak the language of financial capital but also to become better versed in the worlds of human, social, and natural capital. CFOs must acquire not only knowledge of new criteria and new language but also awareness and understanding of the key societal and cultural trends. No longer is it enough to simply follow the money. CFOs must get their brains around the sort of accounting now being done by companies like Puma and Kering (see Chapter Three).

Jean-François Palus, Kering's group managing director and himself a former CFO, explains the CFO's role in implementing an EP&L strategy. "The CFO has the role of an architect and a coordinator," he says. "He or she is at the center of all systemic interactions, has a global vision, and is the most aware of all the implications the project will have on various areas of the company. On another note, the CFO has the ability to say and, sometimes, the duty to say no." Which is where the CFO's reputation for obstruction often comes from.

○ Expanding the Time Horizon for Shareholders

Beyond the C-suite, executives need to help spread the gospel to the wider world of stakeholders — a task that requires clarity, persistence, and stamina. "Too few CEOs can properly tell the story of a better business model to their shareholders and the financial community," Polman observes. "It took us a while, but now our investor base understands it. The story is about our risk aversion, our closeness to society, our reach, how we energize our employees, and finding new business opportunities. Few CEOs are good at this new form of storytelling. We normally have not been trained for that."

Telling the long-term story may be a crucial aspect of this paradigm shift, but so is creating a culture in which the entire organization increasingly gets on board with the change required to think and act long term. "You have to place your company in a framework in which people start to behave differently," Polman insists. "This can involve redesigning compensation systems, running companies in new ways, and talking about it to the wider world. We have made dramatic changes at Unilever that advocate for exactly these things. When it comes to investors, too many CEOs cater to the current investor base."

This means that C-suite executives must find ways to say no to shareholders who constantly demand an extra penny every quarter. They must work to attract new shareholders with lengthier time horizons whose values and philosophies are in line with the organization's longer-term focus. This may well require CEOs and other C-suite and business leaders to rethink their roles. CEOs "must reclaim their title as leaders, both in thought and in practice," argues Polman. "We must demonstrate that C-suite leaders are not selected based on seniority, but on their ability to think differently and to change things for the better that would have otherwise not been changed. This is the true definition of a leader."

It will take collective action on a new scale to stretch our economy's time horizons, with government, C-suite executives, board members, and other stakeholders all coming on board. Stretching time horizons will require everyone to demonstrate the business case as well as the environmental and social cases; to speak the right language (specifically targeted, for example, at CFOs and chief investment officers); to develop more robust information and mine big data; to bridge the knowledge gap (building awareness and skills at the level of the C-suite and board); and to create an enabling environment (aligning business incentives with national and global goals and frameworks). Over time, it also will require leaders to think about financial markets in very different ways.

o Shifting Toward Longer-Term Investing

To have any chance of breaking through, investors also must embrace longer time horizons. InnovaStrat CEO Ram Nidumolu is one of those who stress the need for a more sophisticated approach to financial markets. He notes that there are many different types of investor, all of whom must be approached differently: institutional investors, such as registered investment organizations, including mutual funds, pension funds, endowment funds, investment banking, insurance companies, and closed-end funds; alternative investment vehicles (AIVs), including private equity (PE), venture capital funds, hedge funds, property funds, and so on; and community investment institutions (CIIs), including community development banks and credit unions.

"The motivations can be very different," Nidumolu says. "Money managers of traditional AIVs are more focused on the short term and less likely to embrace socially responsible investment (SRI). A new class of AIVs that are focused on SRI, among them social venture capital, double- or triple-bottom-line private equity, hedge funds, and property funds, is also emerging rapidly. But they will not have the clout and reach (at least in the short to medium term) of institutional investors and CIIs. But institutional investors and CIIs are more likely to embrace SRI, given the right circumstances."

New types of analysts are springing up to bridge the gap. Andy Howard, for example, is cofounder of Didas Research, having previously played a pivotal role in the Goldman Sachs sustainable investment group, GS Sustain. He insists that long-term investing is key to a successful future. "The value of taking a longer term view of stocks has risen as market time horizons have contracted, but new tools are needed to take advantage of that opportunity," he says. The value of longer-term investing has become increasingly apparent, he adds, as "lower-turnover funds have outperformed their higher-churn peers."[4]

None of these changes are guaranteed to happen. It's no secret that equity investors have become increasingly shortsighted in recent decades as shareholders chase extra pennies each reporting season. "Shorter holding periods in themselves are less important than the shift in investment styles that underpins the trend: a growing focus on near-term catalysts, earnings expectations, and the ebb and flow of sentiment," Howard notes, "rather than long-term business fundamentals. Compounding the shorter investment horizons of institutional investors, computerized or systematic trading—much of which is explicitly designed to exploit or hedge short-term price divergence—now comprises more than half the trading volume of major developed exchanges."[5]

At the same time, analysts and other stakeholders seem less inclined to think and project long term. "The proportion providing estimates beyond three years has never been lower," Howard reports. "Where long-term estimates are available, their accuracy is declining. Naively extrapolating past trends provides growth estimates that are almost as accurate as consensus. It is vital to focus on the drivers of sustained growth rather than analyst estimates. Growth is a function of capital allocation decisions and the sustainability and scalability of competitive advantage. Companies that invest a greater proportion of earnings and generate a high return at the margin on those reinvested earnings outgrow peers."[6]

Taking a longer view and aligning with deeper currents in the markets will require business leaders to shift their focus. A key element of this shift, as players like Didas and Generation Investment Management conclude, is that focusing much more carefully on key social and environmental trends — and the economic and political eddies and currents that are forming around them — can provide real long-term dividends.

Among the factors Didas tracks are the rising mistrust of the corporate sector, widening income inequality, intensifying resource constraints, volatile weather patterns, increased access to (and public awareness of) global issues, public sector spending constraints, continuing globalization and industry value chain dis-aggregation, growth in working-age populations in some regions and rapid population aging in others, greater levels of international migration, rising pandemic incidence, and increasing asset owner and investor awareness of such social and environmental factors.

o Rewarding Longer-Term Investors

One possible way forward involves rewarding investors for holding shares over more extended time periods. Frédéric Samama, head of the steering committee for the Sovereign Wealth Fund Research Initiative, notes that "long-term investors are facing an overall ecosystem dedicated to short-termism." With the tide running so strongly in the wrong direction in recent decades, the balance needs to be adjusted.

It may be difficult to imagine markets reversing course in this area. Indeed, according to Long Finance, an initiative that stemmed from an agreement among investment researchers to share environmental, social, and governance information with policymakers, investors, and the public, "current figures put the average holding period for a share of stock at only seven months, a stark contrast to estimates of past holdings ranging between two and ten years."[7]

One solution proposed to counter this kind of potentially destructive short-term investing are loyalty-driven securities. The concept behind these securities is that they reward patient investors. L-Shares can offer additional rewards, such as extra shares or extra dividends, to shareholders who hold their shares for a specified period of time. The reward could be, for example, the right for loyal investors to purchase a warrant for a predetermined number of shares at a set price.[8] These loyalty warrants (or L-shares) can serve as an incentive for investors to remain loyal to a company even if they do not see immediate returns, instead rewarding them for taking a longer view. With such shares, investors can, of course, take profits whenever they choose, but they would benefit from extra financial rewards if they were to stick it out for the long haul.

Such a solution does not come without its own challenges, including that of encouraging widespread market acceptance. Indeed, one recent report found that although "investors, corporations, fund managers, academics, and other thought leaders broadly agree that short-term investment behavior does have a negative impact on the way companies make key decisions, there is little support for the introduction of loyalty rewards (i.e. loyalty dividends, warrants or additional voting rights)."[9]

Although uncomfortable reading, such findings don't negate the potential value of L-Shares or of other approaches evolving beyond this idea. Nor do they mean we should stick with the status quo. Quite the contrary: such findings underscore the need to find new ways to moderate — and ultimately reverse — destructive short-termism. Another, more immediate option is to retool the C-suite and recruit new types of talent to top teams.

o Shuttling Between Timescales

The key skill for breakthrough leaders and teams is to be able to shuttle between different timescales — short, medium, and long. One way to do this is not to try to stuff all these timescales into the brain of one person (for example, the CEO) but to ensure that the entire top team, including the board and the C-suite, can cover all the relevant angles.

The emergence of the new breed of chief sustainability officers, already discussed, is one part of the corporate response. The best of them model new ways of thinking and new ways of framing the future. The agenda these people are coevolving suggests that, uncomfortable though it may be for people trapped in today's capitalism even to think about, tomorrow's breakthrough leaders will need to work out how to sacrifice some short-term gains in order to ensure longer-term outcomes.

In addition to studying what social entrepreneurs are doing, and embarking on experiential learning journeys, expect CEOs and other business leaders to show a growing interest in how family businesses, state-owned enterprises, and sovereign wealth funds think and operate. Such organizations tend to come at the future very differently. (See Chapter Two.)

"Because of the very personal nature of family enterprises and the natural concern for the next generation, long-term sustainability fits easily within the culture of family enterprises," explains Caroline Seow, director of sustainability at the Family Business Network Asia. Successful family businesses, for example, often "emphasize incremental over explosive growth, evolutionary over revolutionary change, and have a deep connection to the communities to which they belong."

Whether running a family business, a nonprofit, or a multi-national powerhouse, breakthrough leaders must think more carefully about how the time horizons they adopt will best sustain their organizations for the long haul. They will also need to work out how to help change the rules of the game—a challenge we turn to in our concluding section.

Conclusion

Get Ready to Break Through

Today's capitalistic economic systems have deep structural flaws that most national governments are ill-equipped to tackle. Thoughtful business leaders, including The B Team, acknowledge that it is time to change the rules of the game—and the cultural context in which key choices are made. They know that doing so represents an immense challenge, not least because the system is composed of manically intertwined economic, social, environmental, technological, and governance strands.

Nevertheless, they are part of a developing consensus that business must become an effective force for system change. One reason: business can experiment and scale solutions in ways—and at a pace—that most governments cannot.

That said, all of this must be set in the context of a global shift away from the relative predictability afforded by the so-called Pax Americana to a future in which the United States is less likely to be either willing or able to serve as a guarantor of the global commons, from sea-lanes to the climate. This splintering of the old security order will have profound implications, including the emergence of what Philip Stephens of the *Financial Times* has called a "fragmented mosaic of global power."[1] With war in the Middle East, tensions in the East and South China seas, climate change, and growing natural resource scarcity, the pressures for conflict, regardless of whether or not we choose to acknowledge them, are intensifying.

The ten steps first outlined by The B Team do not offer a panacea in the context of such immense challenges, but they do suggest an approach by means of which business leaders can begin to shift their organizations—and their industries—onto breakthrough trajectories. Based on a wide range of inputs from business leaders and thought leaders across sectors and around the world, they draw on collective intelligence. They also offer a useful place for those new to the task to start the journey of pursuing the people-planet-profit agenda.

For some leaders, the journey has already begun, but many more must join in—soon—and the pace of progress needs to accelerate dramatically. Indeed, the systemic nature of the crisis is already driving a convergence in the often-competitive and siloed worlds of activism. From Egypt to Turkey to Greece to Ukraine and even to Zuccotti Park, hard by Wall Street, social movements are fusing with political, environmental, and economic movements as people around the world come to recognize the urgent need for change.

"Overall, the trend is for social and environmental movements to merge and ultimately become facets of the same movement," says Kumi Naidoo, executive director of Greenpeace International. "The recent protests in Istanbul are a good example of these movements blending. Many people forget now that 2013's Gezi Park protests [which had broader political and economic implications] were initiated by environmentalists, because of the planned demolition of one of the last remaining public parks in Istanbul. But the general theme is the shrinking of our democratic space and the lack of meaningful consultation between governments and the people they are supposed to represent."

As the physical world shrinks—thanks in large part to new forms of technology that link people around the globe—it becomes more evident that unrest is bubbling up everywhere, particularly as younger generations wake up to the fact that their future and our planet are in peril on multiple fronts. Although most of us think of globalization in economic or business terms, it is increasingly felt in social and environmental terms as well, good, bad, and, too often, ugly.

○ Rewriting the Rules

Changes in language often herald changes in the rules that govern our lives, but changing from an old order to a new one can require a willingness to break the rules. Much admired for his leadership at sea, Admiral Nelson once famously put his telescope to his blinded eye so that he could say he hadn't seen his commander's signals when disobeying orders.

Sometimes, like the man best remembered as the eventual victor in the Battle of Trafalgar, we too must break the rules when they get in the way of progress. However, the nature of today's challenges calls for innovators willing not just to ignore the rules but to change them—and to ensure that the rest of the world then aligns with the new order.

Increasingly, the top echelon of business leaders knows that it cannot long ignore the evidence that a dramatically different market reality is emerging all around. As a result, we see a growing number of projects, initiatives, and platforms designed to build critical mass for change, although much of that effort is currently going into single-issue initiatives rather than driving toward the necessary system change. Too much of the effort also focuses on citizenship, on being good, on being better within the status quo, rather than on ways to retune the economic system — to break through to a more sustainable future quo.

The B Team is one initiative designed to signal the need to jump business efforts way beyond change as usual. Its Plan B agenda is more ambitious than most, but where to begin in translating this agenda into action? Any business leader considering how to change direction would be well advised to kick off with top team briefings on the relevant ideas — and on the new dynamics that are driving those ideas up the leadership agenda.

It would make sense, too, to get a grip on the role of language in both driving and slowing the necessary transitions. The B Team leaders are acutely aware of the power of language to shape the ways in which we think, prioritize, and act. So, too, is David Levine of the American Sustainable Business Council, who concludes that we must wrong-foot the old order by consciously changing the language we use.

"The conventional narrative must be challenged, aggressively and unrelentingly — until it breaks down," he insists. "We must get the media to frame the contest as one between 'old business' and 'new business.' It's a struggle between 'extractive industry' and 'innovative industry,' between 'prosperity for the 1 percent' and 'prosperity for the 100 percent,' between 'short-term exploitation' and 'long-term stewardship.' The media need to hear from, and report on, a new generation of businesses. From those moving way beyond the stale 'either-or' debate — and building a world in which both profit and broader prosperity are delivered."

This "both-and" theme is echoed by other breakthrough leaders. Katherine Collins, founder of Honeybee Capital, notes that today's young people have grown up in "a globally connected world, and they naturally see nuance and gray areas. They live in an 'and' world, not 'either-or.'" At the same time, a growing number of leaders acknowledge the urgent and increasing need for pangenerational alliances. As Collins puts it, "Older people have seen the vast shifts in our planet in recent decades—social, economic, political, environmental—and they have the perspective to assess which of those shifts have been good ones and which have had devastating consequences."

Wrong-footing the old, fading order is a key part of our collective task, as is moving beyond either-or stereotypes to get a better sense of how, on a both-and basis, we can combine the best aspects of the old order with the very different characteristics of the new. We also must get a far better grip on what it is that turns ordinary leaders—and people—into effective agents and champions of breakthrough change.

o Breaking Through

Here are some of the headline messages that today's breakthrough leaders would want to communicate to you, our reader, and to those who are determined to become tomorrow's breakthrough innovators, entrepreneurs, investors, and policymakers.

Accept the Challenge

Those who have already embarked on this journey stress that the first, critical step is to accept the particular challenge (or challenges) that you—and your organization—must tackle.

The work we have spotlighted in such areas as corporate reporting and stakeholder engagement, in effect, are processes designed to allow business leaders not just to operate and innovate but to focus on the real priorities—rather than being forced to try to do everything.

Growing numbers of companies are choosing to zero in on a small number of strategic objectives that are absolutely vital to their future. In the process, many are also embracing stretch targets that take them well beyond what is currently considered to be possible. This sort of ambition will be crucial, but, as you define your aspirations and targets, be careful that you understand the nature and scale of what you are taking on.

Peter Bakker, president of the World Business Council for Sustainable Development, is among the leaders who understand that we're no longer simply talking about responsibility and accountability, but also about the increasingly urgent need for systemic change. "It's a big job and it will take time," he cautions. "But it's the inevitable way. Either we throw away capitalism and start again, or we transform capitalism."

Virtually no one would have expected business leaders to talk in such terms a decade or so ago, particularly the leader of a constellation of hundreds of companies. Once again, however, such people are well positioned to understand that everything in today's world is now connected—and connecting in new ways—with profound implications for all of us, but particularly for those locked into the status quo.

As mainstream business leaders wake up to all of this, expect growing numbers to turn to high-potential change agents in other fields for clues on how to succeed in the new order. People like Gary Cohen, founder, CEO, and president of Health Care Without Harm, who spotlights some of the extremely complex interlinkages he encounters every day of his working life. "Our work is based on the understanding that our campaign needs to be global in nature," he explains. "If we shut down all the medical waste incinerators in the U.S. to eliminate them as a source of dioxin, but China and India built a thousand incinerators, then there would be no gain since dioxin, like many other pollutants, knows no boundaries. The same is true for coal-fired power plants. The health sector needs to raise its voices loud to support divestment in fossil fuels and investment in a healthier energy and economic future."

Like Peter Bakker and Gary Cohen, John Fullerton, a former investment banker and now president of the Capital Institute, recognizes that the time has come to embrace and back new stretch targets. "I resisted the idea that we were at a seminal moment in history for a long time," he recalls. "But I now believe we are at such a moment. We have had many challenges throughout history, but never before have we faced the challenge of running out of planet, with seven billion people and counting, half of whom are barely surviving as it is." The nub of the challenge is that "shifting a growth-driven economy, grounded in compound returns to financial capital invested, is a profound and entirely new challenge," he says. "It will define our legacy to civilization."

This is the sort of language — and prospect — that freezes most busy people in their tracks. But we must ask once again, if not now, when? If not us, who?

History has proven time and time again that those who fear such changes are doomed to failure. "Just as the French aristocracy did not take the structural problems of their society seriously until they reached a moment of massive crisis, it is hard to imagine the titans of the global economy taking structural steps to spread rather than to concentrate their power," says Bob Massie, president of the New Economics Coalition. "But for the sake of the world, that is what they must now do."

There will be intense resistance to breakthrough change, of course, and its champions will not prevail in all sectors or at all times. Nor should we expect truly breakthrough leadership to come from traditional business groups like the U.S. Chamber of Commerce or any other similar business organizations, as David Levine, CEO of the American Sustainable Business Council, stresses. "Such powerful organizations continue to represent unsustainable business practices, ill-suited for the global twenty-first century economy. To level the playing field, business-oriented policy advocates for sustainability are required, making the business case for building a sustainable economy. There is a need for other business voices, capable of matching the U.S. Chamber—and its equivalents around the world—issue by issue."

Businesses, NGOs, and governments have been evolving interesting new styles of partnership in recent years, but very few are yet up to the task of system change. As they engage with new constellations of change actors, however, smart leaders know that this isn't simply a question of signing on to a breakthrough manifesto like Plan B, but an ongoing commitment to an agenda that is going to be increasingly political—and highly volatile at times. New areas of science, new technologies, new business models, and new mind-sets will help keep all of us off balance in the coming decades.

Like it or not, technologies like artificial intelligence, nanotechnology, synthetic biology, and even geoengineering (the use of new technologies to slow and even reverse climate change) cannot be disinvented—and they will continue to evolve. Money will increasingly flow toward these new forms of wealth creation or risk abatement, with enormous consequences for the nature and shape of tomorrow's economy. So now is the time to get involved and engage those who are evolving these new areas of science, technology, and ultimately, business.

Imagine that you are Trevor Maynard, who heads the exposure management and reinsurance team at Lloyd's of London, one of the world's top insurers. His job involves thinking through the worst that could happen—and he has plenty of possible scenarios to choose from. He is interested, for example, in the future of synthetic biology, which he describes somewhat blandly as "genetic modification using a computer."[2] Others might expand on that, noting that one thing synthetic biologists promise (or threaten, depending on your viewpoint) is to create completely new species, unknown to science and to the planet.

Here's what Maynard had to say on that: "When you're tinkering with natural processes, it's not easy to foresee the outcomes. The insurance industry paid £150 billion for the wonder technology that was asbestos. So part of our job is to look out for the next asbestos." Chances are, there will be a fair few candidates.

Commit to Breakthrough Leadership

For those who have accepted the challenge, the next step is to commit to driving transformational change. It may help to understand that this isn't just about huge initiatives that are way beyond the power and resources of individual CEOs and other business leaders. As long as they are well aligned with the direction of change, incremental efforts can be a key part of the process.

"It's not about grand gestures," says Martin Chilcott, chairman and CEO of 2degrees Network, which seeks to build critical mass for change across various business sectors. "For us it's about a different form of breakthrough. We increasingly see that you can drive massive change through thousands of little efficiency-related cuts. It's like undoing the Gordian Knot with a blizzard of razor blade cuts, rather than one big Alexandrian sword strike."

Even some of the more radical campaigners, like Greenpeace's Naidoo, are beginning to acknowledge the impact that businesses can create with their actions. "Some businesses are putting their power to good use," he says. "Google is investing in renewable energy, Nike and H&M are eliminating toxic chemicals from their supply chains, U.K. supermarket giant Sainsbury's is sourcing sustainable seafood and backing marine reserves, and so on. Now, corporate giants like Danone, Philips, and Allianz are demanding an E.U. climate target of 30 percent by 2020 compared to 1990 levels because that would provide certainty for investments. Europe's governments are not yet responding to this call, but ultimately they will have no choice."

Increasingly, it can help would-be breakthrough leaders to think through how they would act if they were among the world's most effective activists. Success, for business too, will often involve building new social and political movements as we work to shift deeply entrenched vested interests away from profit-obsessed bottom-line thinking to more inclusive and integrated forms of management, accounting, and reporting.

Fortunately, a growing number of pioneering change agents are developing tools to do precisely this. James Slezak is a partner at Purpose, a New York–based social business that builds movements driven by people and enabled by technology. He notes that activists and other breakthrough leaders are coevolving a new science of movement building, mixing innovative technology with tools and tactics that in some cases have been in use since the campaigns to abolish slavery through the 1700s and 1800s. Leaders who are committed to pursuing the Plan B agenda could study and learn from the tools, tactics, and technology used by breakthrough movements, both in the past and present.

The B Team is also of one mind when it comes to the challenge of achieving a better balance between the sexes in business. "The empowerment of women has to be a key focus," insists François-Henri Pinault, CEO of Kering. "Most businesses were created by men," Pinault points out, "and corporate cultures reflect that. So there is an urgent need to empower the potential, creativity, and skills of women in business. If we can create a much more favorable business environment, then that helps to empower other women. A virtuous cycle."

We also suggest that you don't give up on governments. Perhaps above all, don't forget how important governments, public policy, and the public sector are going to be in all of this. True, a number of our interviewees were downbeat about the prospects for effective global governance in the near to medium term, including a former Prime Minister, Gro Harlem Brundtland.

We asked her whether it is still possible to shift the global economy toward more sustainable economic and business models in time to avoid major and systemic global crises. "I am not convinced we can, unfortunately!" she replied. "However, I remain an optimist. Many political leaders are aware of the urgency. Business leaders also increasingly realize we have no alternative but to change. Civil society is active—and the social media are conveying key messages. Reinventing government in an interconnected world is no easy task! Still, it must be done. And that process of reinvention also must include private actors, businesses, and civil society, encouraging them all to take a long-term view."

No question, the dysfunctions of governments are many and deep seated. Take the California Environmental Quality Act (CEQA). "A well-intentioned law to curb the damaging effects of development has mutated into a monster," reports the *Economist*.[3] "Almost anyone can file a CEQA lawsuit against any project they dislike; plaintiffs win half of the cases they enter, and when they lose they do not need to cover defendants' fees (the reverse does not apply)." Even radical environmentalists have been heard to argue for reform—and the same is true of the European Union's carbon trading scheme, which has proved largely ineffective in tackling greenhouse gas emissions, while imposing fairly substantial costs on industry.

After a couple of decades of reengineering business, it is time to reengineer every level of government to ensure radically better environmental, social, and governance outcomes, while also boosting the health of our economies.

Leading city governments are starting to engage key elements of the Breakthrough Challenge. In his book *If Mayors Ruled the World*, Benjamin Barber concludes that "cities can save the world." He notes that "rooted in history, [cities] still lean to the future.

As we reach the limits of independence and private markets, they define interdependence and public culture. On a pluralistic planet of difference, they embrace multiculturalism. And as our times plead for innovation, they exude creativity."[4]

To date, the most interesting pan-city initiative has been the C40 grouping, which started life in 2005 and expanded via a partnership in 2006 with President Clinton's Climate Initiative. "The C40 Cities Climate Leadership Group, or C40, is a network of large and engaged cities from around the world committed to implementing meaningful and sustainable climate-related actions locally that will help address climate change globally," explains Terri Wills, director of C40 global initiatives. "As the world's population is increasingly concentrated within cities, they are also becoming the front lines in the battle against climate change. Whether it's urban traffic, energy consumption, solid waste, or the challenge of rising waters or drought—both the causes and effects of climate change focus on the world's largest cities."

This doesn't mean that countries, corporations, or citizens are any less important, only that the real leverage may increasingly be found where the bulk of us are choosing to concentrate.

Get the Internal and External Incentives Right

If accepting the challenge and committing to drive change are key first steps, then getting the incentives right is the next piece of the puzzle. There are at least three levels at which leaders must think about how to incentivize new and improved behaviors: the economy as a whole, the company and its supply chain, and the individual, whether executive, employee, customer, consumer, or investor.

Human beings do good, bad, and ugly things for a variety of reasons. As a result, those whose job it is to manage people in business have learned to use a broad range of financial and nonfinancial incentives to reward good behavior and discourage unwanted behavior. Even so, the more honest practitioners readily admit that the administration of incentives is nowhere near becoming an infallible science. Disasters like BP's Deepwater Horizon oil spill in the Gulf of Mexico or the implosion of financial institutions like Lehman Brothers or the subprime crisis underscore just how complex all this can be, with incentives designed to do one thing inadvertently skewing the outcomes in ways that were never intended.

A small but expanding number of studies have been conducted on how people are best motivated in such areas as product quality, safety, health, environment, and sustainability, although this is an area that needs further research. Similarly, much attention has been lavished on the impact of indexes and awards, with pioneers in the first category including the likes of Dow Jones Sustainability Indexes and FTSE4Good, and in the second category the X Prize. These can galvanize individual leaders, top teams, and entire organizations, but experience suggests that the criteria used for selecting the winners in some indexes — and in a fair few award schemes — may be less robust than they should be.[5]

Because many award schemes carefully shine the spotlight on one particular aspect of a company's activities, there can be surprising results in terms of the companies that win or are celebrated. Once again, this underscores the importance of full transparency — both inside and outside companies and through their supply chains. It also means that we have to be alert to what a business is doing across the ethical, governance, economic, social, and environmental domains.

Digging out the deep truths about particular businesses is very much easier than it was a few decades ago, but it still can be a real challenge, particularly when it comes to efforts to level the playing field by suppressing rule-bending, system-warping behaviors like bribery and corruption. There is a growing need for initiatives that publicly expose malpractice—and that flag those who actively work to slow or subvert the change process.

The scale of malign influence on politicians and governments exerted through mechanisms like campaign finance is too easy to overlook. We must get much better at shining the spotlight on such activities—and at switching the pressure on governments and political leaders to make it easier for them to do the right thing at the right time.

Governments, meanwhile, must get much better at using tax credits and similar financial and regulatory incentives to motivate business to head in the right direction—for example, spurring investment in sectors that potentially can contribute solutions to the Breakthrough Challenge. Tax credits and incentives have already been used to stimulate community revitalization, the retention of city residents, and the reduction of development costs and timescales, as well as to encourage everything from energy efficiency projects to the cleanup and redevelopment of contaminated land. Governments also must avoid the sorts of policy flip-flops that tend to unnerve and discourage many long-term investors.

Among key areas flagged by The B Team leaders as in need of urgent and determined action are the reinvention of tax systems to favor longer-term, more sustainable forms of wealth creation. They want to see the introduction of new approaches to the ownership of businesses, with the expanding B Corp community seen as a useful early step in this direction. They argue the need for a change in the lobbying industry, which they see as in deep need of its own Plan B. Perhaps the ultimate task of all, The B Team leaders also urge the regeneration of the master market discipline of economics to better align it with the needs of the coming decades.

Join Forces — and Keep Us Posted

It's an adage that still resonates: if you want to go fast, go alone; if you want to go far, go in company. If we are to accept the system change challenge, we must find new ways to join forces. Wherever we operate in the global economy, we must build and support many more business organizations that lobby for the new order and against the old. If today's business and industry federations will not do the job, then we must outflank them by creating the next generation of initiatives and platforms.

Jason Kibbey, executive director of the Sustainable Apparel Coalition (SAC), is another leader who is working to rattle the old-order players — and to throw the weight of multiple businesses behind the pioneers of the emergent order. The SAC is developing new tools that could help radically cut the cost of social and environmental assessments right across the apparel sector. The cost of such assessments, he estimates, currently accounts for around 10 percent of the apparel sector's profits — and can represent a significant brake on further progress. Kibbey foresees a future in which many sectors come together to coevolve and use such tools, as the apparel industry is now doing.

We need many more creative approaches like this. One initiative that we particularly like in this space is Sustainia, headquartered in Denmark. Founder Erik Rasmussen experienced a wake-up moment when the government-led 2009 COP15 climate summit in Copenhagen came apart at the seams. After the failure of the summit, Rasmussen tried to figure out what had gone wrong and how the momentum could be restored. Among other things, he explored the cultural dynamics, concluding that there had been a significant language barrier.

"Never has a challenge of this magnitude and importance been communicated so poorly," he notes. "The issues were conveyed in too many different languages. That is not to say English, French, or Spanish. It is to say that science spoke one language, business another, and politicians yet another. The public did not understand any of them, leaving them in the darkness of deepest confusion. No wonder it all failed."

This is not simply a case of different languages, however: we need powerful new narratives, Rasmussen argues. Breakthrough narratives. "There is a real need for a story that holds this scary transition together," he says. "We long for certainty in our planning—and half the time it just doesn't exist. We must learn how to work in real discomfort. A key skill will be to look beyond tired labels of 'NGO,' 'business,' or 'government,' seeing multiple actors with at least some shared goals."

It's time to take flight, break out of our reality bubbles, and wake up to an expanding array of shared goals. "Only a winged soul can bestow wings on other people; and without the soul's wings, a company loses its impetus. It still functions, but it doesn't raise itself into the air to see everything from a different angle," wrote Benedictine monk Anselm Grün in *The Manager and the Monk*, a work coauthored with Jochen.[6]

Few people have gone as far in this direction as Jerry Linenger, a former astronaut and cosmonaut who spent five months on the *Mir* space station. "After logging over fifty million miles in space and orbiting two thousand times, I came to see things a bit differently," Linenger recalls. "I returned with a broader perspective, a tendency toward strategic thinking and toward seeing endless possibilities."

Intriguingly, he likens our progress as a species to the experience of lift-off. "When the space shuttle boosters ignited for lift-off, there was an explosion of so much raw power that it was almost impossible to comprehend how we could actually funnel and direct all that energy," he says. (A bit like the Industrial Revolution, you might conclude.) Until solid rocket booster separation at two minutes into the flight, the ride was wild and chaotic and seemingly out of control. "Then, bang! The boosters separated by means of an explosive charge. The shuttle ride transitioned abruptly from the feeling of traveling inside a stampede of charging buffalo to one more akin to the glide of an eagle."

Linenger concludes that although many of us wish that we could move society more quickly from chaos to pure acceleration, "we are not quite there yet, not quite ready for the transition. But the energy is there, and growing. We need to keep funneling and directing that energy."

That's very much how we and our colleagues in The B Team see the challenge. As they say, we are the people we have been waiting for. Get involved. Help build the movement, creating the critical mass for change. Help coevolve tomorrow's bottom line. Let us know what and how you are doing. This is the ultimate example of a challenge where we all fail — or succeed in breaking through — together.

Notes

Preface

1. See the Breakthrough Capitalism website: http://www.break throughcapitalism.com.

2. Spelled out in greater detail in John Elkington, *Cannibals with Forks: The Triple Bottom Line of Twenty-First Century Business* (Oxford: Capstone/Wiley, 1997).

3. Jochen Zeitz and Anselm Grün, *The Manager and the Monk: A Discourse on Prayer, Profit, and Principles* (San Francisco: Jossey-Bass, 2013).

Introduction: Profit from Tomorrow's Bottom Line

1. Volans, *Breakthrough: Business Leaders, Market Revolutions*, 2013, http://volans.com/wp-content/uploads/2013/02/Break through_Volans_Final.pdf.

2. A number of our interviewees suggested that we reorder "people, planet, and profit" to place the planet first, on the basis that if we screw that up, the effects will cascade through everything else. We chose to stick with the original ordering,

on the basis that The B Team and other champions of change cannot speak to the planet, instead needing to address and persuade people as their primary task.

3. There is a different Plan A, a supply chain management initiative developed by U.K. retailers Marks & Spencer, which for us falls very much into Plan B territory. For more details, see http://plana.marksandspencer.com.

4. We strongly recommend a thorough reading of the work of Lester Brown, both in his influential Plan B series of publications and in the earlier State of the World and Vital Signs series. Les is a towering figure in the landscape — and a continuing inspiration. For a deeper exploration of his life and work, see Lester R. Brown, *Breaking New Ground: A Personal History* (New York: Norton, 2013).

5. For more information, see The B Team website: http://bteam .org/team/.

6. All titles were correct at the time these individuals joined The B Team.

7. Shari Arison, *Activate Your Goodness: Transforming the World Through Doing Good* (New York: Hay House, 2013).

8. Blake Mycoskie, "Founder Blake Mycoskie on the Inspiration Behind TOMS," Forbes.com, February 4, 2014.

9. Terril Yue Jones, "The Made-in-China CEO," *Reuters*, June 2012, http://in.reuters.com/article/2012/06/28/china-ceo -idINDEE85R00V20120628.

10. This is the "4 Keys" formula developed under Jochen Zeitz's leadership while he was CEO of Puma; see http://it .puma.com/news/4keys.

11. Peter Lacy, Tim Cooper, Rob Hayward, and Lisa Neuberger, *A New Era of Sustainability: UN Global Compact–Accenture CEO Study 2010*, June 2010, http://www.unglobal compact.org/docs/news_events/8.1/UNGC_Accenture

_CEO_Study_2010.pdf. For an update, see http://www
.accenture.com/microsites/ungc-ceo-study/Pages/home.aspx.

12. For more information, see "What Is Social Business?"
YUNUS socialbusiness, accessed February 8, 2014, http://
www.yunussb.com/social-business/.

13. For more on the Happy Planet Index, see http://www.happy
planetindex.org.

Chapter 1: Adopt the Right Aspirations

1. California Economic Summit, *2013 Summit Report: Advancing the Triple Bottom Line for All California,* December 2013,
http://www.caeconomy.org/resources/entry/2013-summit
-report.

2. "Elon Musk: The 2013 Businessperson of the Year," *Fortune,*
December 9, 2013.

3. See Volans with JWT, "The Future Quotient: 50 Stars in
Seriously Long-Term Innovation," 2011, http://futurequotient
.tumblr.com.

4. John Elkington, *The Zeronauts: Breaking the Sustainability Barrier* (Oxford: Earthscan/Taylor & Francis, 2012).

5. BRICS are Brazil, Russia, India, China, and South Africa;
MINT comprises Mexico, Indonesia, Nigeria, and Turkey.

Chapter 2: Create New Corporate Structures

1. Michael Townsend, "Sustainable Business Strategy Series—
Part 3: Better by Re-Design," Sustainable Business Lab, May 7,
2013, http://www.sustainablebusinesslab.org/profiles/blogs
/sustainable-business-strategy-series-part-3-better-by-re
-design.

2. Jonathan Moule, "Fresh Index Shows Value of Employee
Share Ownership," *Financial Times,* January 10, 2014.

3. David S. Chesnick and Carolyn B. Liebrand, "Global
300 List Reveals World's Largest Cooperatives," *Rural*

Cooperatives 74, no. 1 (January/February 2007), http://www
.rurdev.usda.gov/rbs/pub/jan07/global.htm.

4. "The Global Co-Operative Sector," Co-Operatives UK,
   accessed February 8, 2014, http://www.uk.coop/worldwide.

5. "How Do I Create General Public Benefit?" Benefit Corp
   Information Center, accessed February 14, 2014, http://
   benefitcorp.net/business operate-as-a-benefit-corporation
   /how-do-i-create-general-public-benefit/.

6. "What Are B Corps?" B Lab, accessed February 14, 2014,
   http://www.bcorporation.net/what-are-b-corps.

7. Innocent website at http://www.chainofgood.co.uk.

8. Michael E. Porter and Mark R. Kramer, "Creating Shared
   Value," *Harvard Business Review*, January 1, 2011, http://hbr
   .org/2011/01/the-big-idea-creating-shared-value.

Chapter 3: Apply True Accounting Principles

1. Jane Gleeson-White, *Double Entry: How the Merchants of
   Venice Created Modern Finance* (London: Allen & Unwin,
   2012).

2. "Introduction to Accounting Principles," Accounting Coach,
   accessed February 14, 2014, http://www.accountingcoach
   .com/accounting-principles/explanation.

3. Gleeson-White, *Double Entry*, 5.

4. Ibid., 8.

5. Robin McKie, "From Fertilizer to Zyklon B: Inventor Who
   Brought Both Life and Death," *Observer*, November 3, 2013,
   http://www.theguardian.com/science/2013/nov/03/fritz
   -haber-fertiliser-ammonia-centenary.

6. Trucost for the TEEB for Business Coalition, *Natural Capital
   at Risk: The Top 100 Externalities of Business*, April 15, 2013,
   http://www.teebforbusiness.org/js/plugins/filemanager/files
   /TEEB_Final_Report_v5.pdf.

7. Ibid.

8. As forecast some years back by SustainAbility: Geoff Lye, *Taxing Issues — Responsible Business and Tax*, 2006. Downloadable from SustainAbility, www.sustainability.com. For more information, see also Geoff Lye, "Tax Avoidance: It May Be Legal But Is It Responsible?" SustainAbility blog, October 16, 2012, http://www.sustainability.com/blog/tax -avoidance-it-may-be-legal-but-is-it-responsible#. Ur27MqVQsSg.

9. Kirk Kardashian, "Measuring Energy," *Fortune*, February 6, 2014, http://money.cnn.com/2014/02/06/technology/energy -points.pr.fortune/.

10. Jen Boynton, "Levi Strauss Develops Triple Bottom Line Khakis," *Triple Pundit*, November 14, 2013, http://www.triple pundit.com/2013/11/levis-develops-triple-bottom-line -khakis/.

11. "Mo Ibrahim Foundation," accessed March 14, 2014, http:// www.moibrahimfoundation.org/overview/.

12. Ibid.

Chapter 4: Calculate True Returns

1. "Economists: What They Do," StudentScholarships, accessed February 14, 2014, http://www.studentscholarships.org /salary/354/economists.php.

2. Jeffrey D. Sachs, "Why We Need a New Macroeconomics," *Huffington Post*, November 18, 2013, http://jeffsachs.org /2013/11/why-we-need-a-new-macroeconomics/.

3. Richard Mattison, "The True Cost of Personal Computers," Trucost blog (for *GreenBiz*), accessed March 10, 2014, http:// www.trucost.com/blog/102/the-true-cost-of-personal -computers.

4. Chaoni Huang, "US$1.9tn — the True Cost of Water," China Water Risk, May 9, 2013, http://chinawaterrisk.org/resources /analysis-reviews/us1-9tn-the-true-cost-of-water/.

5. "Water Security: The Water-Energy-Food-Climate Nexus," World Economic Forum, accessed February 25, 2014, http://www.weforum.org/reports/water-security-water -energy-food-climate-nexus.

6. World Economic Forum Water Initiative, *Water Security: The Water-Energy-Food-Climate Nexus*, World Economic Forum, accessed February 25, 2014, http://www3.weforum .org/docs/WEF_WI_WaterSecurity_WaterFoodEnergy ClimateNexus_2011.pdf.

7. "European Utilities: How to Lose Half a Trillion Euros," *Economist*, October 12, 2013, http://www.economist.com /news/briefing/21587782-europes-electricity-providers-face -existential-threat-how-lose-half-trillion-euros.

8. Prince's Accounting for Sustainability Project, *Future Proofed Decision Making: Integrating Environmental and Social Factors into Strategy, Finance and Operations*, December 2012. For more information, see "A4S Report: Future Proofed Decision Making," http://www.accountingforsustainability.org /embedding-sustainability/a4s-report-future-proofed -decision-making.

9. See "About Us," Generation Investment Management, accessed March 10, 2014, http://www.generationim.com /about/. For more information about Generation's advocacy work on sustainable capitalism, visit the Generation Foundation's library, www.genfound.org/library.

10. "About Impact Investing," Global Impact Investing Network, accessed February 8, 2014, http://www.thegiin.org/cgi-bin /iowa/resources/about/index.html.

Chapter 5: Embrace Well-Being

1. Smitha Mundasad, "NHS-Funded Surf Therapy to Boost Wellbeing," BBC News: Health, November 15, 2013, http:// www.bbc.co.uk/news/health-24744632.

2. Yvon Chouinard, *Let My People Go Surfing: The Education of a Reluctant Businessman* (New York: Penguin Press, 2005).

3. "Measuring National Well-Being," Office for National Statistics, http://www.ons.gov.uk/ons/guide-method/user -guidance/well-being/index.html.

4. John Calverley and Samantha Amerasinghe, *Measuring Sustainable Development*, special report, Standard Chartered Bank Global Research, September 18, 2013. Available at https://research.standardchartered.com/researchdocuments /Pages/ResearchArticle.aspx?&R=109960.

5. Larry Sillanpa, "Happiness Initiative Provides New Measure of Community Well-Being," *Workday Minnesota*, November 4, 2013, http://www.workdayminnesota.org/articles /happiness-initiative-provides-new-measure-community-well -being, February 8, 2014.

6. Lydia Breunig, "Taking Happiness Seriously: Should Tucson Measure Its Subjective Well-Being?" *Arizona Daily Star*, October 8, 2013, http://azstarnet.com/news/blogs/happiness /taking-happiness-seriously-should-tucson-measure-its -subjective-well-being/article_4d07552a-3035-11e3-99ad -001a4bcf887a.html.

7. *World Happiness Report 2013*, Sustainable Development Solutions Network, accessed February 8, 2014, http://unsdsn .org/happiness/.

8. Vivienne Walt, "Why Everyone's Trying to Measure Well-Being," *Time*, May 30, 2012, http://business.time.com/2012 /05/30/why-everyones-trying-to-measure-well-being/.

9. Lauren Drell, "Smaller Than Your Phone, This Device Could Keep You Healthy," Mashable, November 26, 2013, http://mashable.com/2013/11/26/tellspec/#:eyJzIjoidCIsImki OiJfejFhcnJxN2ludWdvbHdldyJ9.

10. *Wellbeing at Work*, Institute of Directors, accessed February 8, 2014, http://www.director.co.uk/content/pdfs/wellbeing _guide.pdf.

11. *The Social Intrapreneur: A Field Guide for Corporate Changemakers*, SustainAbility, April 17, 2008. Downloadable from http://www.sustainability.com/library/the-social -intrapreneur#.Ur7DsqVQsSg.

12. John Elkington and Pamela Hartigan, *The Power of Unreasonable People: How Social Entrepreneurs Create Markets That Change the World* (Cambridge, MA: Harvard Business School Press, 2008).

13. "Education and Economic Opportunity," Skoll Foundation, accessed February 8, 2014, http://www.skollfoundation.org /issue/education-and-economic-opportunity/.

14. Ibid.

15. Wellbeing Enterprises, accessed February 8, 2014, http://www.wellbeingenterprises.org.uk/.

16. Sarah Zielinski, "The Colorado River Runs Dry," *Smithsonian*, October 2012, http://www.smithsonianmag.com/science -nature/The-Colorado-River-Runs-Dry.html.

17. Erika Svendsen, Mary E. Northridge, and Sara S. Metcalf, "Integrating Grey and Green Infrastructure to Improve the Health and Well-Being of Urban Populations," *Cities and the Environment* 5, no. 1, art. 3 (2012), http://digitalcommons .lmu.edu/cgi/viewcontent.cgi?article=1105&context=cate.

18. "Lack of Social Infrastructure Affects Community Well-being," Future Communities, accessed February 8, 2014, http://www.futurecommunities.net/socialdesign/188/lack -social-infrastructure-affects-community-wellbeing.

19. Quoted on the Institute on the American Dream website, accessed February 8, 2014, http://www.behrend.psu.edu /academic/hss/amdream/amerindx.htm.

20. "Mission," Center for a New American Dream, accessed March 9, 2014, http://www.newdream.org/about/mission.

Chapter 6: Level the Playing Field

1. Norman Myers, "Perverse Subsidies," *Encyclopedia of Earth*, August 9, 2007, http://www.eoearth.org/view/article/155197/.
2. Ibid.
3. Damian Carrington, "UK Farming Studies Harm the Public, Study Says," *Guardian*, July 4, 2013, http://www.theguardian.com/environment/2013/jul/04/uk-farming-subsidies-shortchange-public.
4. "Energy Subsidies: Fuelling Controversy," *Economist*, January 11, 2014.
5. Ibid.
6. Matthew Boyle, "Unilever Wants Short, Soapy Showers and Long-Term Investors," Bloomberg Sustainability, July 5, 2012, http://www.bloomberg.com/news/2012-07-05/unilever-wants-short-soapy-showers-and-long-term-investors.html.
7. The three goals are to improve health and well being, to reduce environmental impact and source 100 percent of the company's agricultural raw materials sustainably, and to enhance the livelihoods of people across our value chain. For more information, see "Unilever Sustainable Living Plan," Unilever, accessed March 17, 2014, http://www.unileverusa.com/sustainable-living/uslp/.
8. "FAQs on Corruption," Transparency International, accessed February 28, 2014, http://www.transparency.org/whoweare/organisation/faqs_on_corruption#defineCorruption.
9. "Our History," Transparency International, accessed February 28, 2014, http://www.transparency.org/whoweare/history.
10. Josh Noble, "China's Hotels Shoot Down Their Five-Star Ratings in Bling Battle," *Financial Times*, January 23, 2014.

11. Tom Mitchell and Paul J. Davies, "China Rights Activist Xu Zhiyong Stands Trial in Beijing," *Financial Times*, January 22, 2014, http://www.ft.com/intl/cms/s/0/451cf50a-8304-11e3 -8119-00144feab7de.html.

12. Two key books on this theme are Ian Bremmer, *Every Nation for Itself: Winners and Losers in a G-Zero World* (London: Portfolio Penguin, 2012); and Mark Mazower, *Governing the World: The History of an Idea* (London: Allen Lane, 2012).

13. "Our Organization," Transparency International, accessed February 28, 2014, http://www.transparency.org/whoweare /organisation.

Chapter 7: Pursue Full Transparency

1. Full disclosure: John Elkington has been a member of the EcoVadis advisory board for a number of years.

2. "The IIRC," Integrated Reporting, accessed February 28, 2014, http://www.theiirc.org/the-iirc/.

3. Ibid.

4. "Integrated Reporting," Chartered Institute of Management Accountants, accessed February 28, 2014, http://www .cimaglobal.com/Thought-leadership/Integrated-reporting/.

5. "Earth Overshoot Day," Global Footprint Network, accessed February 8, 2014, http://www.footprintnetwork.org/en/index .php/gfn/page/earth_overshoot_day/.

6. Ibid.

7. "PUMA Completes First Environmental Profit & Loss Account Which Values Impacts at €145 Million," PUMA, November 16, 2011, http://about.puma.com/puma -completes-first-environmental-profit-and-loss-account -which-values-impacts-at-e-145-million/.

8. Ibid.

9. Alan McGill, "Puma's Reporting Highlights Global Business Challenges," PwC, accessed February 4, 2014, http://www

.pwc.com/gx/en/corporate-reporting/sustainability-reporting /pumas-reporting-highlights-global-business-challenges .jhtml.

10. "EP&L," Trucost, accessed March 2, 2014, http://www.trucost .com/environmental-profit-and-loss-accounting.

11. "What Is Social Return on Investment (SROI)?" SROI Network, accessed March 13, 2014, http://www.thesroinetwork .org/what-is-sroi.

12. Ibid.

13. Sara Olsen, "The Problem with SROI," Skoll World Forum, June 2, 2009, http://skollworldforum.org/2009/06/02/the -problem-with-sroi/.

14. "BT's End-to-End Carbon Footprint, Including Scope 3 Carbon Emissions," BT, accessed March 14, 2014, http://www .btplc.com/Betterfuture/NetGood/OurNetGood Methodology/BT0056-02_BT_Scope_3_carbon_emissions _v02a.pdf.

15. "Big Business, Big Data, Big Sustainability," Carbon Trust, October 31, 2013, http://www.carbontrust.com/news/2013 /10/big-business-big-data-big-sustainability.

16. "Ford Uses Big Data to Drive Sustainability," *Environmental Leader*, October 28, 2013, http://www.environmentalleader .com/2013/10/28/ford-uses-big-data-to-drive-sustainability/.

17. "Ford Embracing Analytics and Big Data to Inform Eco-Conscious Decisions, Stay Green," Ford News Center, October 25, 2013, http://corporate.ford.com/news-center /press-releases-detail/ford-embracing-analytics-and-big-data -to-inform-eco-conscious.

18. Sustainable Business News, "UPS Advances Sustainable Operations with Big Data," *GreenBiz* blog, November 11, 2013, http://www.greenbiz.com/blog/2013/11/11/ups-advances -sustainable-operations-big-data.

19. Johan Rockström and Anders Wijkman, *Bankrupting Nature: Denying Our Planetary Boundaries* (Oxford: Routledge, 2011). For more information, see also http://www.routledge.com /books/details/9780415539692/.

20. "Circular Economy," Ellen MacArthur Foundation, accessed March 3, 2014, http://www.ellenmacarthurfoundation.org /circular-economy.

21. "The Circular Model," Ellen MacArthur Foundation, July 8, 2013, http://www.ellenmacarthurfoundation.org /circular-economy/circular-economy/the-circular-model-an -overview.

22. "Interactive System Diagram," Ellen MacArthur Foundation, July 8, 2013, http://www.ellenmacarthurfoundation.org /circular-economy/circular-economy/interactive-system -diagram.

23. "Managing Net Positive," Kingfisher, accessed February 8, 2014, https://www.kingfisher.com/netpositive/index.asp ?pageid=213.

24. "Conversations," Kingfisher, accessed February 8, 2014, https://www.kingfisher.com/netpositive/index.asp?pageid= 171.

25. "The Business Benefits," Kingfisher, accessed February 21, 2014, http://www.kingfisher.com/netpositive/index.asp ?pageid=177.

Chapter 8: Redefine Education

1. Delia Bradshaw and Laurent Ortmans, "MBA Graduate Pay Doubles in Downturn," *MBA* (blog), *Financial Times*, January 26, 2014, http://www.ft.com/intl/cms/s/2/c6f6e4f8-8351-11e3 -86c9-00144feab7de.html.

2. Emma Boyde, "A Degree of Relevance for the 21st Century?" *Financial Times*, July 15, 2013, 10.

3. CIPD, *CIPD/Hays Resource and Talent Planning Survey 2013*, 2013. Downloadable from http://www.cipd.co.uk/pressoffice /press-releases/war-talent-increases-threefold-labour -turnover-slows-down-190613.aspx.

4. Francesco Di Meglio, "Going Green: MBA Sustainability Programs," *BloombergBusinessweek*, April 17, 2012, http:// www.businessweek.com/articles/2012-04-17/going-green -mba-sustainability-programs.

5. Joel Stonington, "B-Schools' New Mantra: Ethics and Profit," *BloombergBusinessweek*, November 10, 2011, http:// www.businessweek.com/business-schools/bschools-new -mantra-ethics-and-profits-11102011.html.

6. "About Us," Beyond Grey Pinstripes, Aspen Institute Center for Business Education, accessed February 9, 2014, http:// www.beyondgreypinstripes.org/content/about-us.

7. Clay Voorhees and others, *Gen Y and Sustainability*, Michigan State University, 2010, http://news.msu.edu/media /documents/2010/01/7f991e2a-9b1d-4949-abf0-0f34c471 cd7d.pdf.

8. "About Net Impact," accessed February 8, 2014, http:// netimpact.org/about-net-impact.

9. Patrick Jenkins, "High Pay Fed Ethical 'Vacuum' at Barclays," *Financial Times*, April 4, 2013.

10. Ben Bland, "Executives Shown a Fresh Perspective on Sustainability," *Financial Times*, January 13, 2014.

11. Sarah Murray, "Sustainability Lessons from the Boardroom," *Business Education* (blog), *Financial Times*, October 31, 2011, http://www.ft.com/intl/cms/s/2/ca14464e-fefb-11e0-9b2f -00144feabdc0.html.

12. Ibid.

13. "About Us," Beyond Grey Pinstripes.

14. Ibid.

Chapter 9: Learn from Nature's Model

1. Unless otherwise noted, all quotations of Janine Benyus in this chapter are from "What Do You Mean by Biomimicry?" Biomimicry Institute, accessed February 22, 2014, http://www.biomimicryinstitute.org/about-us/what-do-you-mean-by-the-term-biomimicry.html.
2. "The Industrial Symbiosis at Kalundborg, Denmark," Indigo Development, accessed February 9, 2014, http://www.indigodev.com/Kal.html.
3. "The Q&A: Michael Pawlyn, Lessons of Design Learned from Nature," *Prospero* (blog), *Economist*, November 9, 2011, http://www.economist.com/blogs/prospero/2011/11/qa-michael-pawlyn.
4. Biomimicry Europe, Innovation & Finance Summit, accessed February 9, 2014, http://www.biomimicry.ch.
5. "What Is Natural Capitalism?" Co-Intelligence Institute, accessed February 9, 2014, http://www.co-intelligence.org/P-naturalcapitalism.html.
6. Dan Barber, "How I Fell in Love with a Fish," TED, February 2010, http://www.ted.com/talks/dan_barber_how_i_fell_in_love_with_a_fish.html.
7. "The Eden Project Biomes," Exploration, accessed February 9, 2014, http://www.exploration-architecture.com/section.php?xSec=21&xPage=1&jssCart=71e1d0c6a69adbcd4b3c375d87755d0b.
8. "Biomimicry," Biomimicry 3.8, accessed February 9, 2014, http://biomimicry.net/about/biomimicry/.
9. "The 15 Coolest Cases of Biomimicry," brainz, accessed February 9, 2014, http://brainz.org/15-coolest-cases-biomimicry/.
10. "Lufthansa Tests the Effects of Shark Skin in Flight," Learning from Nature, Lufthansa Group, February 5, 2013,

http://www.lufthansagroup.com/en/press/news-releases
/singleview/archive/2013/february/05/article/2337.html.

11. Hans Schürmann, "Learning from Nature," Siemens, accessed
9, 2014, http://www.siemens.com/innovation/apps/pof
_microsite/_pof-spring-2012/_html_en/facts-and-forecasts
-learning-from-nature.html.

12. Quoted in John Elkington and Pamela Hartigan, *The Power
of Unreasonable People: How Social Entrepreneurs Create
Markets That Change the World* (Cambridge, MA: Harvard
Business School Press, 2008). Adapted from George Bernard
Shaw, "Maxims for Revolutionists," *Man and Superman*
(Cambridge, MA: University Press, 1903; Bartleby.com,
1999), www.bartleby.com/157/6/html.

13. "Can Products Be Manufactured Without Producing Any
Waste?" Q1–Q10: The InterfaceFLOR Story in 10 Questions, InterfaceFLOR U.K., accessed March 15, 2014,
http://www.interfaceflor.co.uk/assets/bespoke/interfaceflor
-story/swf/interfaceStory.swf.

14. "GE Previews SXSW: A Biomimicry Expert Makes His
Debut," *GE Reports*, March 10, 2011, http://www.gereports
.com/ge-previews-sxsw-a-biomimicry-expert-makes-his
-debut/. This page is no longer available.

15. Tom Vanderbilt, "How Biomimicry Is Inspiring Human
Innovation," *Smithsonian*, September 2012, http://www
.smithsonianmag.com/science-nature/How-Biomimicry-is
-Inspiring-Human-Innovation-165592706.html.

16. Joel Makower, "Biomimicry's Growing Web of Opportunity,"
GreenBiz blog, September 16, 2013, http://www.greenbiz.com
/blog/2013/09/16/biomimicry-spins-web-opportunity-0.

17. "About the J. Craig Venter Institute," accessed March 5, 2014,
http://www.jcvi.org/cms/about/overview/.

Chapter 10: Keep the Long Run in Mind

1. Dominic Barton and Mark Wiseman, "Focusing Capital on the Long Term," *Harvard Business Review*, January-February 2014, 45–51.

2. John Elkington, "Rio+20 Was Grim, but Optimism and Innovation Could Turns Things Around," Guardian Sustainable Business, July 4, 2012, http://www.guardian.co.uk/sustainable -business/sustainability-with-john-elkington/rio-20-grim -optimism-innovation-turn-things-around.

3. Full disclosure: John Elkington has been a member of Nestlé's Creating Shared Value advisory board for several years.

4. Andrew Howard, *A Path Through the Woods* (London: Didas Research, November 26, 2013), 1.

5. Ibid., 4.

6. Ibid., 1.

7. Stephanie Hay, "Loyalty Shares Aim to Change Long-Term Investment Patterns," Long Finance, June 12, 2013, http:// www.longfinance.net/groups7/viewbulletin/155-loyalty -shares-aim-to-change-long-term-investment-patterns.html.

8. Patrick Bolton and Frédéric Samama, "L-Shares: Rewarding Long-Term Investors," Social Science Research Network, November 1, 2012. Downloadable from http://papers.ssrn .com/sol3/papers.cfm?abstract_id=2188661.

9. "Mercer 'Loyalty' Shares Research Indicated Consensus on Negative Impact of Short-Termism," Mercer, December 18, 2013, http://www.mercer.com/press-releases/loyalty-shares.

Conclusion: Get Ready to Break Through

1. Philip Stephens, "Riches and Risk: Welcome to the World of Tomorrow," *Financial Times*, January 10, 2014, http://www .ft.com/intl/cms/s/0/50a64ed2-779f-11e3-807e-00144feabdc0 .htm.

2. Emma Jacobs, "What Could Possibly Go Wrong?" *Financial Times*, June 28, 2013, 12.

3. "The Not So Golden State," *Schumpeter* (blog), *Economist*, January 25, 2014, http://www.economist.com/news/business /21594967-all-silicon-valleys-vibrancy-california-can-be -lousy-place-do-business-not-so.

4. Benjamin R. Barber, *If Mayors Ruled the World: Dysfunctional Nations, Rising Cities* (New Haven, CN: Yale University Press, 2013), 358–359.

5. For more information, see SustainAbility *Rate the Raters* reports. Downloadable at http://www.sustainability.com /projects/rate-the-raters.

6. Anselm Grün and Jochen Zeitz, *The Manager and the Monk: A Discourse on Prayer, Profit, and Principles* (San Francisco: Jossey-Bass, 2013), 169.

Acknowledgments

We thank **Sir Richard Branson** and all our other friends and colleagues at Virgin Unite (particularly **Jean Oelwang**), The B Team, Puma SE, Kering SA, and Volans (particularly **Sam Lakha**) for supporting us in what turned into a fairly major project.

We thank **Karen Murphy** and **John Maas** at Jossey-Bass for their commitment to the project and for their editorial support, and we thank **Doris Michaels** of DSM Agency for placing the book and **Kelli Christiansen** for her help in shaping the final text.

We thank all those who have helped develop the Breakthrough Capitalism initiative since 2011, including **Colin le Duc** of Generation Investment Management, **Jamie Arbib** and **Kelly Clark** of Tellus Mater, **Lynelle Cameron** of Autodesk, **Paul Ellingstad** of HP, and **David Christie** of the Value Web. And we are grateful to all those who have helped organize follow-up events in cities like Berlin, Bogotá, London, Nairobi, Potsdam, Singapore, and Toronto.

We thank **Elaine Elkington** and other family members and friends for their tolerance, wise counsel, and help in keeping the locomotive on the rails.

Our biggest debt, however, is to our interviewees. Any errors of commission or omission are ours alone. They included **Shari Arison** (owner, Arison Group; member, The B Team); **Peter Bakker** (president, World Business Council on Sustainable Development); **David Barber** (cofounder and president, Blue Hill Farm Restaurant); **Janine Benyus** (founder, Biomimicry 3.8); **David Blood** (managing partner, Generation Investment Management); **Peter Brabeck-Letmathe** (chairman, Nestlé); **Gro Harlem Brundtland** (former prime minister of Norway; chair, World Commission of Environment and Development; deputy chair, The Elders; honorary member, The B Team); **Susan Burns** (cofounder and senior vice president, Global Footprint Network); **Kathy Calvin** (president and CEO, United Nations Foundation; member, The B Team); **Dave Chen** (cofounder and principal at Equilibrium Capital; board member, B Lab); **Martin Chilcott** (founder and CEO, 2degrees Network); **Niels Christiansen** (former vice president, public affairs, Nestlé); **Gary Cohen** (founder, president, and executive director, Health Care Without Harm); **Katherine Collins** (founder and CEO, Honeybee Capital); **Rodolphe d'Arjuzon** (cofounder and global head of research, Verdantix); **Paul Druckman** (CEO, International Integrated Reporting Council [IIRC]); **Debra Dunn** (associate professor, Stanford d.school; board member, B Lab); **Rodolphe Durand** (GDF SUEZ professor of strategy, HEC Paris); **Robert G. Eccles** (professor of management practice, Harvard Business School); **Jed Emerson** (chief impact strategist, ImpactAssets); **Linda Fisher** (vice president, safety, health and environment, and chief sustainability officer, DuPont); **Betty Sue Flowers** (professor emeritus, University of Texas); **John Fullerton** (president, Capital Institute); **Fadi Ghandour** (founder and CEO, Aramex; founding partner, Maktoob.com); **Mark Goyder** (founder director, Tomorrow's Company); **Michael Green** (executive director, Social Progress

Imperative); **Mauro Guillén** (director, Joseph H. Lauder Institute, University of Pennsylvania); **Derek Handley** (founding CEO, The B Team); **Pamela Hartigan** (director, Skoll Centre for Social Entrepreneurship, Saïd Business School, University of Oxford); **Denis Hayes** (president, the Bullitt Foundation; organizer, Earth Day, 1970); **Andy Howard** (cofounder and head of SRI research, Didas Research); **Jonathan Hsu** (former CEO, Recyclebank, New York); **Arianna Huffington** (president, and editor-in-chief, The Huffington Post Media Group; member, The B Team); **Ioannis Ioannou** (assistant professor of strategy and entrepreneurship, London Business School); **Nina Jablonski** (distinguished professor of anthropology, Pennsylvania State University); **Jean-Pierre Jeannet** (emeritus professor of global strategy and marketing, IMD); **Antony Jenkins** (group chief executive, Barclays); **Hannah Jones** (vice president of sustainable business and innovation, Nike); **Jason Kibbey** (executive director, Sustainable Apparel Coalition); **Paul King** (CEO, UK Green Building Council); **Lise Kingo** (executive vice president, Novo Nordisk A/S); **Gail Klintworth** (chief sustainability officer, Unilever); **Casper ter Kuile** (cofounder, Campaign Bootcamp); **Guilherme Peirão Leal** (cofounder and board member, Natura; founder, Instituto Arapyaú; member, The B Team); **Jim Leape** (former director-general, WWF International); **Jeremy Leggett** (chairman, Solarcentury; chairman, Carbon Tracker Initiative); **Lindsay Levin** (founder and managing partner, Leaders' Quest); **David Levine** (CEO and cofounder, American Sustainable Business Council); **Ernst Ligteringen** (chief executive, Global Reporting Initiative); **Jerry Linenger** (former astronaut and cosmonaut); **Peggy Liu** (chairperson, JUCCCE [Joint US-China Collaboration on Clean Energy]); **Bob Massie** (president, New Economics Institute); **Richard Mattison** (chief executive, Trucost); **Bill McKibben** (founder, 350.org); **Doug Miller** (founder and chairman, GlobeScan);

Sir Mark Moody-Stuart (chairman, Hermes Equity Ownership Services; former CEO, Royal Dutch Shell; former chairman, Anglo-American); **Kumi Naidoo** (executive director, Greenpeace International); **Jane Nelson** (director, Harvard Kennedy School's Corporate Social Responsibility Initiative); **Ram Nidumolu** (founder and CEO, InnovaStrat); **Jean Oelwang** (CEO, Virgin Unite); **David Orrell** (mathematician and author); **Sally Osberg** (president and CEO, Skoll Foundation for Social Entrepreneurship); **Jean-François Palus** (group managing director, Kering); **François-Henri Pinault** (CEO, Kering; member, The B Team); **Paul Polman** (CEO, Unilever; member, The B Team); **Jørgen Randers** (professor of climate strategy, BI Norwegian Business School); **Erik Rasmussen** (founder and CEO, Monday Morning; founder, Sustainia); **Robert Rubinstein** (CEO, TBLI Group); **Frédéric Samama** (head, Steering Committee, Sovereign Wealth Fund Research Initiative); **Caroline Seow** (executive director, Family Business Network Asia); **Amam Shishmanian** (CEO, World Gold Council); **Feike Sijbesma** (CEO and chairman, management board, Royal DSM); **James Slezak** (partner, Purpose); **Sir Tim Smit** (cofounder and chief executive, development, the Eden Project); **Ulrich Steger** (professor; former Alcan Chair for Business and the Environment, IMD); **Frederick Chavalit Tsao** (chairman, IMC Pan Asia Alliance Group [IMC Group] and IMC Corp; president, Family Business Network [FBN] Asia); **André van Heemstra** (chairman, supervisory board, Koninklijke Brill N.V.; chairman, steering group, Netherlands Network Global Compact; vice chair, supervisory board, Academy of Business in Society; former board member and personnel director, Unilever); **Stewart Wallis** (executive director, New Economics Foundation); **the Most Reverend Justin Welby** (archbishop of Canterbury; member, 2012 Parliamentary Commission on Banking Standards); **Gail Whiteman** (professor of sustainability, management, and climate change, Rotterdam School of Management, Erasmus

University); **Lorie Wigle** (vice president, security fabric program, Intel subsidiary McAfee); **Terri Wills** (director, global initiatives, C40); **Zhang Yue** (founder and chairman, BROAD Group; member, The B Team); and **Muhammad Yunus** (founder, Grameen Bank, Bangladesh; member, The B Team).

Thank you all.

About the Authors

John Elkington (Twitter: @volansjohn) has worked for forty years in the environmental, sustainability, and social innovation fields. He has cofounded four companies (Environmental Data Services in 1978, John Elkington Associates in 1983, SustainAbility in 1987, and Volans in 2008), sits on more than twenty boards or advisory boards, and is a founder-member of The B Team advisory board. He has now authored or coauthored nineteen books, including the million-selling *Green Consumer Guide*. Among the terms he is responsible for are *environmental excellence* (1984), *green growth* and *green consumer* (1986), *triple bottom line* (1994), *People, Planet & Profit* (1995), *Future Quotient* and *future quo* (2011), and *the global C-suite* (2012).

His first involvement in the field was as a fundraiser, at age eleven, for the newly formed World Wildlife Fund (WWF) in 1961. He now sits on WWF U.K.'s Council of Ambassadors. Rather than focusing on NGOs or governments, however, Elkington has focused on working with business, through markets, on some of the defining challenges of our time.

In 2004, *Business Week* described him as "a dean of the corporate responsibility movement for three decades." In 2008, the *Evening Standard* named him among the "1000 Most Influential People" in London, describing him as "a true green business guru" and as "an evangelist for corporate social and environmental responsibility long before it was fashionable." In 2009, a CSR International survey of the top one hundred CSR leaders placed him fourth, after Al Gore, Barack Obama, and the late Anita Roddick of the Body Shop, and (startlingly) alongside professor Muhammad Yunus of the Grameen Bank.

His work has been acknowledged by awards from the United Nations, the Skoll Foundation, *Fast Company*, the American Society for Quality, the International Society of Sustainability Professionals, and the Rockefeller Foundation, among others.

Jochen Zeitz (Twitter: @JochenZeitz) is cochairman and president of The B Team. He is a director at Kering (formerly PPR) and chairman of the board's sustainable development committee, after having been CEO of the Sport & Lifestyle division and chief sustainability officer (CSO). Previously, he served eighteen years as chairman and CEO at Puma. He is a board member of Wilderness Safaris and has been a member of the board of directors of Harley-Davidson since 2007, recently also becoming the chair of Harley-Davidson's newly created sustainability committee.

Zeitz began his professional career with Colgate-Palmolive in New York and Hamburg, joining Puma in 1990 — and in 1993 was appointed chairman and CEO, becoming the youngest CEO in German history to head a public company. He spearheaded the worldwide restructuring of Puma, which was in financial difficulties, turning the company from a low-priced, undesirable brand into one of the top three brands in the sporting goods industry.

In May 2011, he launched Puma's EP&L account, which puts a monetary value to a business's use of ecosystem services across the entire supply chain. In October 2010, he was appointed chief sustainability officer at PPR (now Kering), and soon after launched PPR HOME, a new sustainability initiative across the global brands (for example, Gucci, Balenciaga, and Stella McCartney) of the group, which operates four interconnected strands: leadership, ecology, humanity, and creativity.

In 2010, Zeitz cowrote *The Manager and the Monk: A Discourse on Prayer, Profit, and Principles* with Anselm Grün, a Benedictine monk. The book has been translated into nine languages and covers such topics as sustainability, the economy and prosperity, culture, values, success, and responsibility.

He has received the *Financial Times* Strategist of the Year award three times. In 2004, he was awarded the Federal Cross of Merit of Germany, and, in 2010, the German Sustainability Foundation gave him an award for sustainable strategy.

For more information, please visit:

www.bteam.org (for more on The B Team)
www.breakthroughcapitalism.com (for more on the Volans
    Breakthrough Program)
www.volans.com (for more on other work by Volans)
www.johnelkington.com (for blogs on the book's roll-out)

Index